Divining the Self

signifying (on) scriptures

VINCENT WIMBUSH, GENERAL EDITOR

Signifying (on) Scriptures, a project of the Institute for Signifying Scriptures at the Claremont Graduate University, invites and challenges scholars from different fields and disciplines to engage the phenomenon of signifying in relationship to "scriptures." The focus of these works is not upon the content meaning of texts but upon the textures, signs, material products, practices, orientations, politics, and power issues associated with the sociocultural phenomenon of the invention and engagement of scriptures. The defining interest is how peoples, especially the historically dominated, make texts signify as vectors for understanding, establishing, and communicating their identities, agency, and power in the world.

Divining the Self

A STUDY IN YORUBA MYTH AND HUMAN CONSCIOUSNESS

VELMA E. LOVE

THE PENNSYLVANIA STATE UNIVERSITY PRESS
UNIVERSITY PARK, PENNSYLVANIA

LIBRARY OF CONGRESS CATALOGING-IN-PUBLICATION DATA

Love, Velma E., 1949–
Divining the self : a study in Yoruba myth and human consciousness / Velma E. Love.
p. cm. — (Signifying (on) Scriptures)
Summary: "Explores the dynamics of African American engagements with the Holy Odu, the unwritten sacred scriptures of the West African Ifa Orisha tradition. Examines the experiences of selected practitioners, focusing on the ways in which the divinatory narrative and associated mythology impact self-understanding and worldview"—Provided by publisher.
Includes bibliographical references and index.
ISBN 978-0-271-05405-6 (cloth : alk. paper)
ISBN 978-0-271-05406-3 (pbk. : alk. paper)
1. African Americans—Religious life.
2. Yoruba (African people)—Religion—Influence.
3. Ifa (Religion)—United States.
4. Orishas.
I. Title.
II. Series: Signifying (on) Scriptures.

BL2532.S5L68 2012
299.6833300973—dc23
2012015636

Printed in the United States of America
Published by The Pennsylvania State University Press,
University Park, PA 16802–1003

The Pennsylvania State University Press is a member of the Association of American University Presses.

It is the policy of The Pennsylvania State University Press to use acid-free paper. Publications on uncoated stock satisfy the minimum requirements of American National Standard for Information Sciences—Permanence of Paper for Printed Library Material, ANSI Z39.48–1992.

For CHIEF ADENIBI S. AJAMU (1940–2009)

CONTENTS

PREFACE AND ACKNOWLEDGMENTS

One fateful day I walked into a botanica on 125th and Broadway in New York City with an anthropologist friend. Looking around, I noticed that this tiny shop was filled with an assortment of candles, flowers, herbs, incense, figurines of the Catholic saints, books, pamphlets, and other types of spiritual supplies. I listened intently as my friend engaged the shop owner in a lengthy conversation about dreams, readings, and spirit energy. When there was a brief pause in the conversation, the owner—a *santos,* or Santeria priest, I later realized—turned to me and said, "Why are you so quiet?" "I don't know what to say. I don't know anything about what you are talking about," was my reply. He looked at me intently for a second and said, "You think too hard." I said, "Well . . . I'm a graduate student. I just finished my exams . . . so, yes, I've been thinking hard." He then told me that I needed to cleanse my aura. I didn't have the faintest idea of what he meant, and I responded, "Well, how would I do that?" He prescribed a special black soap and gave me the recipe for an herbal wash. This was my first informal "reading."

Processing this experience over lunch with my friend, I learned that the botanica was more than it appeared to be: it was a place where people came not only to purchase supplies but also to seek guidance. I learned that the shop owner practiced a religious tradition called Santeria, which could be traced back to Cuba and ultimately to the Yoruba culture or the Ifa/Orisha tradition of West African origin, and that there was a corpus of unwritten scriptures, known as the Odu, that was associated with divination, popularly known as readings. I pondered over this new information for the next few days, and out of sheer curiosity, I used the black soap and the herbal wash prescription. Much to my amazement, I found that using the soap and the five-herb wash left me feeling refreshed and energized, and the whole experience had really piqued my curiosity. And so began my investigation of African American engagements with the unwritten sacred text known as the Odu.

This brief reflection offers a glimpse of the botanica as a cultural site where "readings of world" take place on a regular basis. It also offers a glimpse of an "experiential, participatory epistemology" in process. The researcher's knowledge of the world of the botanica was constructed, in part, through intimate involvement, not passive observation. That experience of knowing fueled my quest to understand the Yoruba spiritual tradition, but it also taught me an important lesson about performance ethnography and the construction of knowledge. My intellectual curiosity, coupled with this embodied way of knowing, was the beginning of what later became a formal research study. This book is basically a documentation of my study—of the questions I sought to answer, the methods I engaged, and what I learned along the way.

The investigative trail led me to Oyotunji African Village in Sheldon, South Carolina, a community established in 1970 by practitioners of Yoruba religion/culture who had moved there from New York City. At Oyotunji Village I met and interviewed the initial consultant who introduced me to many of the practitioners who eventually became a part of my study. Some of the people to whom I was referred lived in New York City but maintained contact with residents of Oyotunji and visited periodically to attend religious festivals and ceremonies. Some of them were themselves former residents of the village. Some were first-generation practitioners, while others were second-generation. They ranged in age from twenty to ninety, and in educational levels from grade school to college, with comparable income levels. A few earned their livelihood as full-time priests, while many held regular jobs as professionals in their fields. Regardless of whether they were young or old, male or female, educated or uneducated, or lived an urban or a rural lifestyle, divinatory readings were an important part of their lives. The chapters that follow open a window onto the world of African American Yoruba culture—the mythology, cosmology, and worldview that shapes the lives of practitioners, the scriptures they live by, and the meanings they find through their engagements with the Odu.

This book would not have been possible without the assistance of many. I extend my deepest gratitude and most sincere appreciation to the people who contributed to the completion of this project. I especially thank those who participated in this study by sharing their personal stories and private lives with me. A very special thanks goes to Vincent L. Wimbush, director of the Institute for Signifying Scriptures, who saw value in my ideas before they were fully formed, and Jacob K. Olupona, who welcomed me as one of his students though I never sat in his classroom. To the friends and colleagues who have walked with me throughout the journey, helping in every conceivable way, I am eternally grateful. I especially thank Sylvester L. Johnson and Sharon V. King for editorial assistance; Betty Bolden, Joy R. Bostic, Marian David, Renee K. Harrison, Violet Dease Lee, Heather A. Nicholson, Robin L. Owens, Lawrence J. Toliver, and Carmen Williams for the constant support, understanding, and encouragement that helped sustain me; and my brother, Leon A. Love Sr., for accompanying me on my first trip to Oyotunji Village.

I am grateful to The Fund for Theological Education, the United Methodist Women of Color Scholars, the Wabash Center for Teaching Theology and Religion, and the Interdenominational Theological Center's Womanist Scholars Fellowship Program for financial resources that in part funded this work.

Finally, I extend a special thanks to Patrick Alexander, the director of The Pennsylvania State University Press, who believed in this project from its first incarnation; to the anonymous readers whose critique made this a much stronger work; and to my most ardent supporters and greatest teachers, my daughter, Tamu Toliver Lewis, and my son, Lee Thompson Young.

A NOTE ON THE TEXT

A number of Yoruba-language words appear in this manuscript without diacritical marks. The Anglicized spellings are consistent with those often used by African American Yoruba practitioners. I believe that the contextual meanings of these words will be clear to readers, regardless of their familiarity with the Yoruba language.

The term *Odu* refers to the entire living scripture, which comprises 256 individual *odus,* or divinatory signs.

Variant spellings of words and names are retained in direct quotations from other scholars and practitioners.

INTRODUCTION

I was not a stranger to rural South Carolina when I traveled to the town of Sheldon in 1999. I had driven down rough and bumpy dirt roads on sunny days before—winding roads with potholes and gutters, roads lined by trees and underbrush, wildflowers, and weeds. But this road was different, for I was not sure where it would lead. I heard the beat of a drum in the distance, and I saw that the road came to an end just ahead. The hand-lettered sign read, "You are now leaving the United States of America." As I looked around, I felt as though I were in a different place and time. Noticing the official "STOP" sign at the entrance to the gate, I parked beside several other vehicles. A twelve-foot-high archway in the tan stucco front wall marked the entrance to Oyotunji African Village, South Carolina, and the beginning of my journey with the Holy Odu—the unwritten, living scriptures of the Yoruba people of West African origin.

Established in 1970, Oyotunji Village was a child of the Black Consciousness movement. The early founders sought not just a physical space but also a psychological space in which they could feel rooted and grounded. From this space, they could summon from some deep inner source the material for a reconstructed memory (or perhaps not a memory at all, but an imaginative construction) of a way of being in the world, a way that felt safe and secure and meaningful. Now, more than thirty years later, I had come to this very spot to listen, to watch, and to learn.

A fifty-something-year-old African American man, dressed in a light-colored dashiki with matching drawstring pants, greeted me at the gate. I introduced myself as a graduate student conducting research on African American engagements with sacred texts. "Could I talk with the priest?" I asked, not knowing that there were many priests. Without ever suggesting that my question was uninformed, he simply responded, "Which one?" Before I could answer, he gestured to another gentleman nearby and said, "Oh, here's Chief Ajamu. He's a good person for you to talk to." Chief Adenibi S. Ajamu, an African American man who appeared to be in his sixties, was one of the senior priests and founders of the Village. His head was shaved clean, and he wore traditional African attire, a light tan robe with matching pants and sandals. A multicolored beaded diviner's bag hung from his shoulder, and he had a book in his hand. I later learned that the book contained commentary on the Odu.

My first two-hour conversation with Chief Ajamu explored the basic tenets and practices of the Ifa/Orisha tradition, which I introduce here but will describe later in greater detail. The word *orisha* (a singular and plural term) refers to gods, divinities, and forces of nature. Oyotunji Village was founded by a group of African American Yoruba practitioners from New York City who wanted to "uncover the saints"—that is, to reveal the orisha behind the camouflage of the Catholic icons used in Santeria. Santeria, the Cuban version of the West African Ifa/Orisha tradition, survived because enslaved Africans secretly worshipped the orisha while seeming to venerate the Catholic saints (see chapter 1). When African Americans embraced the Orisha tradition as part of the black nationalist movement in the 1960s, some of the newly initiated priests decided that they no longer needed to conceal their beliefs. A small group, led by Oba Oseijeman Adelabu Adefunmi I, moved to South Carolina and established Oyotunji African Village, which marked the beginning of Yoruba revivalism in America. "Oyotunji" means that Oyo, the ancient African kingdom, "rises again" or "wakes up." In the words of Chief Ajamu, "We wanted to build a monument to our African past, lest we forget. But the ancestors tricked us. . . . They got us down here, and we had to learn a lot in order to survive."

As I reflected on Ajamu's comment, several questions surfaced. What African past? Did the founders have Yoruba ancestors? Did it matter? With an estimated population of forty million people in West Africa, the Yoruba are one of the largest ethnic groups in sub-Saharan Africa. The largest concentration of the population is in the southwestern region of Nigeria, though other parts of West Africa, including the Republic of Benin, Togo, and Ghana, also have large Yoruba populations. While not all Yoruba people practice the indigenous Ifa/Orisha tradition, many people of non-Yoruba ancestry, including African Americans, throughout the Diaspora have voluntarily embraced it. In his account of Yoruba culture, Kola Abimbola, a practicing priest and author, finds that close to 100 million people of different racial backgrounds—living in Argentina, Australia, Brazil, Colombia, Cuba, France, Italy, Jamaica, Japan, Mexico, Trinidad and Tobago, the United Kingdom, the United States, and Venezuela—are linked to the tradition.[1]

Given the expansive and relational nature of the Ifa/Orisha tradition, it is difficult to know exactly how many practitioners there really are, especially because some practitioners combine multiple religious identities and may merge Yoruba practices with those of Catholicism, Islam, or Protestant Christianity. Citing census data from Cuba and Brazil, professor of religion and bestselling author Stephen Prothero notes that the often-quoted figure of 100 million Yoruba worldwide may not be a realistic estimate, but he argues that the number certainly runs into the tens of millions, with at least 25 million in West Africa, 10 to 25 million in Brazil, 2 to 3 million in Cuba, and a few hundred thousand in the United States. He names the Yoruba religion as number six in what he considers to be the eight rival religions of the world.[2]

Historian Albert J. Raboteau reminds us that the enslaved Africans in North America were from many different parts of Africa and embraced various cultures and traditions, including, among others, those of the Mandinka, the Yoruba, the Ibo, the Akan, and the Bakingo. He notes that the Senegambia region also supplied a large number of Muslim Africans to the Atlantic slave trade. "It is important to remember," he writes, "that no single African culture or religion, once transplanted in alien soil, could have remained intact: it was inevitable that the slaves would build *new* societies," blending their social experiences and their cultural traditions.[3] In spite of this diversity, though, as Raboteau points out, a thread of continuity was located in the style of ritual performance, including singing, drumming, and dancing, along with a general perspective on the world.

The Yoruba religion thus appears with different faces throughout the Diaspora—indeed, its fluidity is one of its defining characteristics. Whether the face is that of Ifa in West Africa, Lucumi in Cuba, Candomblé in Brazil, or Shango in Trinidad, to name a few, the shared unwritten sacred "text" is the Odu—or, more specifically, one or more of the 256 *odus*, or divinatory signs, which are the means through which the orisha speak to the human condition. In the Yoruba worldview, the invisible world of spirit energies, consisting of ancestors, deities, and the unborn, is as real as the visible world. Through a life-force energy known as *ashe* that permeates and infuses all things, members of the human, animal, plant, and mineral kingdoms are connected. Each odu accessed through divination is said to provide an awareness of how these invisible energies affect an individual or communal situation. The divination narrative also provides a prescription for restoring balance when an imbalance has been detected.

Divining the Self focuses on African American engagements with the Odu, the storied environment, the divination narratives, and the related rituals, ceremonies, and outcomes. It embraces the "signifying scriptures" model of focusing on people and their engagements with the literature deemed sacred rather than on the literature in isolation. In exploring the questions of African American engagements with the Odu, I have also explored questions of what it means to take a performative, interactive approach to the study of scriptures from any tradition, along with questions of what it means to "scripturalize." My quest took me beyond classes at Union Theological Seminary and Columbia University, beyond the libraries, bookstores, museums, and archives, and ultimately into several communities of practitioners, including those in New York City as well as Oyotunji Village. I quickly learned that there was no road map for the work I wanted to do—no clearly stated methodology for the study of unwritten scriptures. Text-centered biblical criticism, even in its most radical form, did not work for the study of the Odu, a living body of knowledge that encompassed an alternative way of knowing. While anthropologists had used performance theory in the general study of religion, scholars of religion had not themselves engaged such models in the study of scriptures. Vincent Wimbush introduced the "signifying scriptures" approach, a model that shifted the focus from texts to worlds of experience and practice.[4] Although no structural guidelines for this model existed, it provided a conceptual compass for me, and I used it to find my way as I began to traverse the unfamiliar terrain of the Holy Odu. Perhaps, as one practitioner later suggested, the warrior orisha were working on my behalf (Esu/Elegba opening the roads, Ogun clearing the path, Ochoosi gathering the *ashe*-capacity to make things happen), for I stumbled upon Dwight Conquergood's performance paradigm and found in it a lifeline.

Conquergood suggests that performance studies scholars must "recuperate from performance some oppositional force, some resistance to the textual fundamentalism of the academy, must use performance as a lever to de-center . . . the textualism that pervades dominant regimes of knowledge."[5] Noting the difference between a textual paradigm and a performance paradigm, Conquergood further suggests that a "textual paradigm privileges distance, detachment, and discourse as ways of knowing . . . while a performance paradigm insists upon immediacy, involvement, and intimacy as modes of understanding."[6] It is the experiential, interactive, intimate focus that makes the performance paradigm well suited not only to a study of African American engagements with the Odu, but also to the range of meaning-making activities involved in the scripturalizing practices of any tradition. As Norman Denzin notes, "In this interactionist epistemology, context replaces text, verbs replace nouns, structures become processes. The emphasis is on change, contingency, locality, motion, improvisation, struggle, situationally specific practices and articulations, the performance of con/texts."[7]

In this study I take up the challenge of determining what it means for the scholar of religion to study scripture as both text and performance. As noted above, my approach draws from Vincent Wimbush's concept of signifying scriptures and uses Joseph Roach's and Dwight Conquergood's ideas of a performance paradigm for focusing on the Ifa Odu literary corpus, the Yoruba sacred literature, as engaged by African Americans in the construction of self and world. Wimbush's signifying scriptures model places its primary focus "not upon the content meaning of texts, but upon textures—upon the signs, material products, practices, orientations, politics and power issues associated with the socio-cultural phenomenon of the invention and engagement of scriptures."[8] The African American engagements with Yoruba "scriptures" provide an excellent case study for examining these performative aspects of scriptures.

We can safely say of Wimbush's model what Joseph Roach, in *Cities of the Dead*, says of his performance paradigm: It "does not require historians to abandon the archive, but it does encourage them to spend more time in the streets."[9] Roach suggests that what we popularly refer to as "culture" is a process of remembering and forgetting, a process that is expressed in a variety of performance events, ranging from the stage show, the carnival, and the festival to the rituals of everyday life. He further explains, "To perform in this sense means to bring forth, to make manifest, and to transmit. To perform also means, though often more secretly, to reinvent" (11).

It is in this sense that I use the term "perform" in my investigation of the sacred Odu. How does the Odu "perform" in the lives of African Americans immersed in the Orisha tradition? What does it bring forth, make manifest, transmit? How and in what ways does it reinvent? In the creation of a category he calls "circum-Atlantic performance," Roach uses the word "orature" to point to something that transcends the conventional categories of orality and literacy, suggesting that various modes of communication and forms of expression have interacted over time to produce such a hybrid (ibid.). Those forms of expression that he categorizes as "orature"—a term borrowed from the Kenyan novelist and theatrical director Ngũgĩ wa Thiong'o—include "gesture, song, dance, processions, storytelling, proverbs, gossip, customs, rites, and rituals" (ibid.). These modes of communication are important aspects of scriptural interpretation by religious practitioners.

In his study of New Orleans Mardi Gras street performances, Roach recognizes the interdependence of orature and literature, suggesting that some things may be recorded in the literature, but the literary record is only part of the story; behaviors are remembered, too, and put into practice through orature, or performance. He suggests that through the Mardi Gras Zulu Parade, an African cultural pattern in the form of the trickster archetype (Esu) is reinvented in the social context of New Orleans. Such "restored behaviors" enacted and performed "function as vehicles of cultural transmission" (ibid.). In the case of African American engagements with the Odu, we could question whether such behaviors are "restored" or whether they are in fact imaginative constructions. The memory, performance, substitution paradigm that Roach describes as the genealogy of performance is closely akin to Wimbush's concept of signifying scriptures, an interactive process of making meaning by appropriating, revising, embellishing, and expressing "scriptures" through a variety of forms and creative acts. In this study of African American engagements with the Odu, I argue that the scripturalizing practices serve to construct and reconstruct self and world.

Representation is an important aspect of this analysis, and the sign theory developed by Charles Sanders Peirce is helpful as a theoretical framework for this discussion. As Robert Preucel describes it, Peirce's understanding of "synechism as the connectedness of all life and semiosis as the process of growth" fits well with the Ifa/Orisha worldview.[10] Peirce's typology of signs includes the icon, the index, and the symbol, each functioning in a slightly different way.[11] The icon is based on the characteristics of an object; for example, in orisha iconography, the machete represents the orisha Ogun's ability to cut away obstacles along the journey of life. The index functions as an indicator, in the way that the "signature," or coded markings, of each odu represents a corpus of stories, sayings, or proverbs that further explicate the situation in question. The odu Ogunda is associated with the orisha Ogun, which indicates, as Peirce points out, how one sign is connected to another sign. The symbol, as defined by Peirce, obtains its character from the ideas associated with it through convention. The orisha Ogun, for instance, symbolizes a warrior energy that cuts through obstacles. The *oriki* (praise songs), prayers, dances, gestures, rituals, and ceremonies for Ogun, as representational actions, add to the association of ideas or conventions that determine the meanings assigned to Ogun. It is in this way that I use the term "symbol" in the discussion of the Odu and the Ifa/Orisha tradition.

Though more in line with the Saussurean tradition, Sherry Ortner, a feminist anthropologist and student of Clifford Geertz known for her work on symbols, meaning, and power, provides a system of classifying and grouping symbols that is helpful in examining the rich universe of symbols in Ifa/Orisha worship. Grouping key symbols into two categories—summarizing symbols and elaborating symbols—Ortner posits that summarizing symbols "sum up" or express for adherents, in an emotionally powerful way, what an experience means to them.[12] In this schema, sacred symbols in the broadest sense, as objects of reverence, are summarizing symbols. Elaborating symbols, on the other hand, help order experience and provide vehicles for sorting out complex feelings and ideas.

The summarizing symbols of Ifa/Orisha worship include the *igbamole* (the great calabash of creation), the top half of which represents *orun* (the heavens or the invisible world), and the bottom half of which represents *aye ile* (the visible world or the inhabited earth). Figure 1 shows a drawing of the calabash on a wall that encloses the "Market Place" and courtyard at Oyotunji Village. This symbol represents the Yoruba worldview, one in which the theme of parallel worlds plays a major role. Much of what goes on in the ritual practice has to do with the connection between the invisible world of spirit and the inhabited world.

On a nearby wall in Oyotunji Village another key symbol, the *opon Ifa* (divination board), is drawn (see fig. 2). It, too, represents the universe. When the diviner casts the *opele* (chain) or throws the cowrie shells, the odu is said to "drop from Heaven," suggesting that the odu travels from the invisible realm, or *orun*, to the visible realm (earth). For the *babalawo* (literally, "father of mysteries," or priest), the *opon Ifa* is also a summarizing symbol, representing not only the universe but also the worldview of practitioners. It is on this board, this sacred symbol of the universe, that

Figure 1 Calabash drawing by Keeland Bankhead, courtyard wall, Oyotunji Village, August 2004. Photo: author

the babalawo traditionally writes the "signature" of the odu. The image at the top center of the border represents Esu/Elegba, commonly referred to as the "trickster god." But as Henry Louis Gates Jr. reminds us, on a deeper level, "Esu . . . assumes his role of interpreter and implicitly governs the process of translation of these written signs into the oral verse of the *Odu*. . . . Esu is our metaphor for the uncertainties of explication, for the open-endedness of every literary text."[13] Esu/Elegba is described by adherents as the "divine messenger," the one who opens roads, inner and outer; the one who links the visible and invisible worlds; and the one who may either garble or clarify communications. It is no wonder then that Esu/Elegba, the cement figure with cowrie-shell eyes, nose, and mouth, is part of the sacred arsenal of every practitioner. I discuss the significance of this elaborating symbol in chapter 2.

The inscription in the circle represents the signature of the odu Ogbe Oshe, marked on the *opon Ifa*. Since I was unable to speak directly with the priest/artist who created this drawing, I can only speculate as to why this odu was selected for display in the courtyard. According to the description provided in *The Sacred Ifa Oracle*, one of the reference books used by several of the priests who participated in the study, Ogbe Oshe speaks of "good news and achievements that call for celebration."[14] The display of this

Figure 2 *Opon ifa* drawing by Keeland Bankhead, courtyard wall, Oyotunji Village, August 2004. Photo: author

particular odu seems to be consistent with the idea of the transformative power of Yoruba spiritual technology, the capacity to reinvent and re-create self and world. Ogbe is an odu in which the orisha Obatala speaks. Oshe is the odu of the orisha Oshun. Obatala and Oshun are considered the guardian orisha of Oyotunji Village.

The signature in the circle and the remaining 255 odus are elaborating symbols. Each of the odus, representing a potential energy that may or may not have manifested in a person's life, helps provide an awareness of the complex forces at work in a given experience. As noted above, the odus are considered the voice of the orisha, and each odu is linked to a number of proverbs and stories. A priest performs divination for a client to shed light on a situation and determine what story the client is living; the priest may also ascertain what can be done to change the story. As one priest/diviner phrased it, "It is the diviner's job to read the client's life story and help him/her to rewrite it."[15] This "reading" of the client's life generally includes identifying the client's "guardian orisha." Everyone has a dominant orisha, a particular "head" or "consciousness." Applying Ortner's schema, the orisha might also be considered both a summarizing as well as an elaborating symbol. As a summarizing symbol, the orisha represents a personality archetype, a divinity, a force of nature, an aspect of God, or an energy matrix. The diviner generally identifies the orisha that is "speaking" in the odu that falls. As an elaborating symbol, the orisha helps the practitioner understand what it means to be influenced by particular energies and what strategies to use to bring about desired changes. What Ortner refers to as the "key scenario," another type of elaborating symbol, is, in this context, the ontological journey of life. Strategies for living a successful life (i.e., a life of balance and harmony) are embedded in the *apatakis* (mythical tales), the *oriki* (praise songs), and the odus as well as in the rituals and ceremonies.

Every *yawo*, or first-year initiate, learns the apatakis, objects, colors, *oriki*, dances, numbers, feast days, attributes, and personality characteristics associated with each orisha.[16] In effect, the initiate is taught the "orature" of orisha "performance" in everyday life, and part of this performance is related to the sacred Odu. The apatakis are passed on verbally from one generation of priests to another, and they are what anthropologists Elizabeth Fine and Jean Haskell Speer refer to as an epistemological verbal performance, "a way of knowing self, culture, and others more completely."[17] Fine and Speer, drawing from Erving Goffman's work on the presentation of self in everyday life, suggest that "stories of self and community that have been repeated often enough to become artfully shaped performances are clear indices of a person's sense of identity."[18] Yoruba orisha archetypes, some of which I discuss in chapters 5 and 6 below, exemplify such performances. The Ifa Odu literary corpus, accessed and activated through divination, serves as the basis for understanding one's self in relationship to the world—and because it is highly adaptable to individual situations, it presents an opportunity for exploring not only how "scriptures" are produced but also how they "perform" in culture. The odus and related texts have survived primarily through oral tradition and performance. Although in recent years much of the material has been collected and published, the tradition still may be characterized as oral, for many apatakis are transmitted verbally. Though it is not uncommon to see African American diviners consulting a book to check the technical accuracy of their readings, this living body of knowledge is dynamic and changing. According to my consultants, there are two definitive texts used by the babalawo. *The Sacred Ifa Oracle*, by Afolabi A. Epega and Philip John Neimark, contains an English translation of all 256 odus of the ancient oral tradition, along with interpretations for contemporary life; William Bascom's *Sixteen Cowries: Yoruba Divination from Africa to the New World* is another collection used extensively throughout the orisha priesthood. But all diviners are encouraged to memorize the odus, the corresponding configurations, and at least one story or proverb for each. A popular companion book for priests in the *dilogun* system is *The Secrets of Afro-Cuban Divination: How to Cast the Diloggún, the Oracle of the Orishas*, by Ócha'ni Lele. While these texts are consulted for technical information, a number of factors are considered in interpretation, including the intuition of the diviner as well as the age, gender, social circumstances, and cultural environment of the client. These factors indicate that the meanings are found in the people and their relationship with the "scriptures," not in the content or form of the scripture, whether oral or written. As one priest aptly described it, "It is a knowledge system based on flesh and blood, spirit and thought."

The divination ritual includes prayers and the manipulation of palm nuts (*ikin*), the divining chain (*opele*), or cowrie shells (*carico*) to arrive at a configuration that represents one of the 256 odus. Epega and Neimark describe the odus as "complex organisms, waiting to be meshed uniquely with each client's personal energy."[19] In the Ifa/Orisha tradition, the individual is considered to be part of a very complex system of energies that make up the universe. The task of the diviner is to identify the individual's degree of harmony with these energies and to prescribe rituals or offerings to create balance when an imbalance exists. Each odu represents an energy system and carries with it hundreds of tales that have accumulated in the oral tradition through thousands of years. In effect, each time the *ikin* or cowries are cast, a new "scripture" is written. The personal energy of the client mixes with an odu to produce meaning.[20] Thus, the meaning of an odu is not inherent but socially constructed, based on the culture, the personal experiences of the client, the knowledge and awareness of the diviner, and the mythology represented by the odu.[21]

As a participant observer, I have documented my own experiences as a client and have been astonished at the diviner's knowledge and interpretation of the Odu. I have observed other clients with the diviner and have watched their expressions of amazement when the divination narrative is given, and I have read published and unpublished accounts of personal experiences with the integration of the divination narrative into one's life.[22]

Methodology

Using ethnographic methods, including in-depth interviews, participant observation, and document analysis, I sought to determine how the sacred scripture of the Yoruba, i.e., the Odu, functions to construct and reconstruct self and worldview. Toward this end, I conducted research in two field sites: Oyotunji Village, South Carolina, and New York City, including Brooklyn and the Bronx. These sites have an organic relationship. The founder of Oyotunji Village, Oba Oseijeman (born as Walter Eugene King), established the Yoruba Temple in New York City in the 1960s before migrating to the South and establishing the Village in 1970. My initial visit was in 1999, nearly thirty years after the founding. Over the course of the next four years, I returned for field research several times. One of my Oyotunji consultants referred me to several practitioners from New York, which led to other contacts and additional interviews. I discovered that many of the people I met had, at one time or another, lived at, trained in, or traced their priestly lineage to Oyotunji.

In South Carolina, Oyotunji Village's minister of foreign affairs, Chief Ajamu, served as the initial contact and consultant. For years, Ajamu served as an "ambassador" to practicing communities throughout the United States and was recognized nationally and internationally as a senior Ifa priest with a wealth of knowledge on Yoruba traditions, both in Africa and in the Diaspora. Initial contacts in New York City included a senior Yoruba priest, Lionel F. Scott (Babalosha Odufora), to whom Ajamu referred me. Odufora taught a series of classes entitled Introduction to Yoruba Religion/Culture, which provided an excellent opportunity for participant observation.[23] I also observed Chief Ajamu conducting a divination session in Atlanta, Georgia.

During the course of the study, I interviewed twenty-one practitioners, twelve male and nine female. Using an open but focused approach, I followed an interview guide, but not a structured interview schedule.[24] This narrative inquiry process allowed respondents to tell their stories, relay their feelings, and report experiences within social contexts, rather than simply answering factual questions.[25] Generally, the participants chose the location for the interview. The interviews lasted from forty-five to ninety minutes. I met people where they were most comfortable, sometimes in their homes or in restaurants, parks, gardens, or at the site of local orisha festivals. Questions designed to facilitate simultaneous reflection and reporting prompted participants to consider their personal experiences with the sacred Odu and to share their stories. One of the objectives was to determine how such "scriptures" have been internalized, embodied, and actualized during significant life events.

The second strategy, participant observation, allowed me to supplement the interview data and get at the "phenomenon" on an experiential basis.

Participant observation operates on a different epistemological basis, one uniquely suited to the nature of the inquiry. I was not privy to all of the rituals and ceremonies that were held behind closed doors; I was considered an *aleyo*, a non-initiated person, and participants were reluctant to discuss some topics with me. Still, none of the stories I heard or the books I read provided the same level of insight and understanding that I gained from actively participating in Yoruba rituals and ceremonies. This immediate, intimate way of knowing generated the multisensory material needed for developing a portrait that captures the experiential and performative aspects of engaging scriptures in life.

Performance theory, literary reception theory, and ritual theory are part of the framing of the study as well as the analysis and reporting. Of particular relevance, in this regard, is Edward Bruner's theory of the anthropology of experience, suggesting that meaning always lies in the here and now of performed texts.[26] Though divination narratives are central to this study, I also have, to a lesser extent, researched other means of engaging the sacred, including meditation, trance possession, dream interpretation, music, dance, chanting, and the visual arts, as each has a relationship with the Odu. The following chapters weave strands of personal narrative, myth history, and contextual observations into a tapestry that reflects the dynamic, embodied nature, material culture, and storied environment of African American engagements with the Holy Odu.

Readings from the Elders

The scholars who have significantly affected my thinking regarding the work of Yoruba "sacred texts" include Wande Abimbola, Ócha'ni Lele, Laura S. Grillo, and Afolabi A. Epega and John Philip Neimark. Wande Abimbola, a well-known and widely respected Ifa priest and scholar of religion, focuses on the structural and technical aspects of the Ifa literary corpus, the system of divination through which it is accessed, and its cultural background. His discussion of the Yoruba concept of destiny and *ori* is most helpful to my work. According to Abimbola, the *ori* is the personal god that guides each individual's "inner head." Therefore, "one can say that when a person goes to consult Ifá all he is doing is finding out the wishes of his Orí. Ifá is merely a mouthpiece, an intermediary between the inquirer and his Orí. . . . The role of the gods is to aid Orí in leading every person to his destiny in life."[27] From this perspective, the odus accessed through divination offer the client a reading of "self" as well as a prescription for recasting "self."

In the system described by Abimbola, the babalawo engages the Ifa corpus. However, in the Lucumi system, a Cuban version of the Yoruba tradition and one also practiced by African Americans, the *babalosha* (the priest of one of the orisha) engages the Afro-Cuban *dilogun* corpus, a related body of literature. I have relied heavily on the work of Ócha'ni Lele, a practitioner since 1989, for an understanding of the *dilogun* and its corresponding system of cowrie-shell divination.[28] Lele writes for the diviner, providing detailed instructions on "opening, reading, and closing the oracle," as well as extensive information on the body of lore that surrounds each odu in the Lucumi system. He speaks not only to the mechanics of manipulating the divination implements but also to the metaphysics and meaning inherent in the coded configurations of shells that are cast on the mat. Lele describes the Odu as a dynamic principle and active force:

> Remember that although each odu contains all the facets of our faith and lives, they are not stagnant, unchanging, mere collections of sacred stories and scripts conceived centuries ago. Each of these letters is alive in the universe and in our lives. They are organisms of energy, creatures of symbiosis awaiting connection with our own human energies as they are opened on the mat. . . . The sacred shells reveal the forces at play in an adherent's life, and these energies are redefined and placated as the orisha priest manipulates the letters in an attempt to help his client evolve. Diloggún is an oracle, yes; yet it is also a long, arduous road to change and personal transformation. It is the heart of Santería and New World orisha worship.[29]

Lele's remarks reflect the dynamic, symbiotic nature of scripture as a religious and cultural phenomenon active in the lives of adherents. The extensive glossary and the examples of recorded readings with the *dilogun* also make Lele's work valuable.[30]

Epega and Neimark's definitive collection of the 256 odus is a crucial resource for understanding the intricate system of signs, symbols, and practices that function as an integral part of the priest/practitioner's life. As they explain,

> In casting a specific odu for a client, the babalawo meshes the universal energy and wisdom of the particular odu with the specific

> circumstances facing the client. It is this "marriage" between the truth of the odu and the reality of the client that creates a unique and individual interpretation of current and future events. This synergy between client and odu provides the dynamic that keeps Ifa as accurate and important today as it was thousands of years ago.
>
> Unfortunately, most Western anthropologists . . . who have studied Ifa have always viewed the sacred odus as *divine text*—unalterable, literal, written in stone. . . .
>
> Far from being literal and unalterable, the odus are alive. They are complex organisms, waiting to be meshed uniquely with each client's personal energy before being "written."[31]

Epega and Neimark have described a system that is based on "scripture as human activity," the dynamic phenomenon that is the focus of this study.

In like manner, Laura S. Grillo argues that divination, as a means of constructing reality, establishes the contextual ground that facilitates a discourse around identity, authority, and meaning, shaped according to the contours of real life. She points to the role of the sacred Odu in the cultural construction of identity and in the negotiation of selfhood and destiny. Grillo's focus on divination as a "visual canon" that serves as a resource for stimulating the imagination for the recasting of experience in the light of culture is an especially useful concept.[32] Her study, based primarily on archival sources, offers an excellent basis for a comparative examination of contemporary ethnographic sources.

Only a few scholars of the Yoruba religion have focused specifically on African Americans. In 1979, Carl M. Hunt published the first history of Oyotunji Village. A narrative centered on Walter Eugene King (Oba Oseijeman), this history tells the story of the founders during the first ten years of life in the Village. Hunt describes in detail the personal experiences, struggles, hardships, and conflicts of the "Black nationalists" who initially moved from New York City to South Carolina to establish a community where they could practice the Yoruba religion according to ancient African traditions.[33] Some of the founders of the community Hunt wrote about participated in my study and referred to his work as an accurate account of the early years of the community's development.

Following the publication of Hunt's *Oyotunji Village*, most of the scholarly work on Yoruba religious practices in the United States focused primarily on Santeria as practiced in Afro-Cuban and Latin communities.[34] Then, in 1997, Mary Curry's study of the African American Yoruba community in New York City was published. Curry's ethnographic study focuses primarily on the social structure and the practical aspects of the religion.[35] She also points to the African American emphasis on "re-defining" Santeria. Curry suggests that identity issues are of major concern for African American practitioners, but her study stops short of an in-depth examination and analysis of such concerns. By focusing on "Odu outcomes," *Divining the Self* picks up where Curry left off. This study also builds on the work of Steven Gregory, whose research on Santeria focuses on aspects of cultural resistance. His emphasis on the religion as an alternative means of affirming and renegotiating ethnic identity and cultural heritage among Latinos and African Americans is relevant to my investigation of the scripturalizing practices associated with the Odu.[36] Maxine Kamari Clarke's ethnographic study of Yoruba traditions practiced at Oyotunji Village and in Oyo, Nigeria, has also offered important insights into the social and psychological dynamics at work among African American Yoruba practitioners.[37]

The popular material written by practitioners—especially John Mason, Lionel F. Scott, Ócha'ni Lele, Awo Fá'lokun Fatunmbi, and Aina Olomo—has proven key to my study. Mason, a priest of Obatala in Brooklyn, has written extensively about the practical aspects of orisha worship. He is a musician, writer, and photographer who is known for his collaboration with Gary Edwards in *Black Gods: Òrìṣà Studies in the New World,* which describes the orisha archetypes, as well as his *Ìdáná Fún Òrìṣà: Cooking for Selected Heads,* recipes for ritual foods; his translation of the *oriki, Orin Òrìṣà: Songs for Selected Heads;* and his *Four New World Yoruba Rituals.* Mason is one of the African American elders in the religion and was cocurator, along with Robert Farris Thompson, of the popular visual art and artifacts exhibition Beads, Body, and Soul: Art and Light in the Yoruba Universe. He has devoted much time and energy to preserving the culture.

Lionel F. Scott (Babalosha Odufora), also an African American elder and an initiated priest of Obatala since 1960, focuses on the apatakis, which he describes as stories and sayings that symbolically express the moral teachings and principles of the culture.[38] He has published only a few of the apatakis in the vast repertoire passed on to him in *Tales of Ancestors and Orishas* and *Beads of Glass, Beads of Stone.* He has also written about the spiritual technology and metaphysics of orisha worship in *The Amber Talisman.* Awo Fá'lokun Fatunmbi, a Euro-American initiated priest of Ifa trained in Nigeria, writes as an initial outsider who had a difficult time grasping and understanding the African worldview. Fatunmbi's discussion of the Ifa proverbs, folktales, and prayers associated with each odu provides insight into the ways in which the "scriptures" of a people reflect their understanding of the relationship between self and world.[39]

Aina Olomo, an African American priestess of Shango, presents a strong critique of the practitioners who have "hung a verbal African belief system on a biblical structure." She suggests that too many have written about the mechanics of divining and the content of the oracles rather than the "main features that are involved in living the Odus."[40] She is concerned that Yoruba religion in the West might become another book religion. In her words, "The new priests . . . are reading books and quoting oracles as if they were biblical scripture. They have not yet realized that having a written document does not determine spiritual truth, and replacing spiritual exploration with memorized quotations is not the ancient Yoruba way to conceptualize a spiritual perception. . . . It is not the way indigenous people whose spirituality is based in nature attain their spiritual vision."[41] Olomo's critique opens the way for my exploration of exactly how the Yoruba adherents, both Old World and New, "live the odus" and how they "attain their spiritual vision."

Presentation

In chapters 1 and 2, I discuss the mythology surrounding the origin of the sacred Odu. I also briefly survey the social and historical circumstances under which African Americans embraced orisha worship and the Odu, examining the conjuring traditions among enslaved Africans in America as well as the cultural nationalist ideology that influenced many of the first-generation practitioners. These chapters illustrate reclamations of self through the imaginative reconstruction of a cultural landscape. As Fine and Speer express it, "When the cultural or physical landscape is torn, or when circumstances wrench people from their homelands, performance provides a way to recover that physical space through the imaginative reconstruction of a cultural landscape, either through words and gestures or through the combined narrative of words and textile art."[42]

Chapters 3 and 4 look at Yoruba "scriptures" as both unwritten text and performance. Giving attention to the vast body of oral literature and the divinatory process through which it is engaged in the production of meaning and worldview, I examine related practices, events, and behaviors by highlighting specific case studies of practitioners in South Carolina and New York. I also discuss the Odu corpus as part of a psycho-social-spiritual healing system and examine the diagnostic and prescriptive aspects of divination along with the role and function of art, altars, icons, and other symbols. The *ita* reading, performed as part of initiation rites and ceremonies, and the subsequent negotiation of selfhood and destiny take center stage here. The ita reading provides a snapshot of the client's life—past, present, and future—with prescriptions for balance and harmony.[43]

Chapters 5 and 6 pay particular attention to the feminine energy principle represented by selected orisha. I examine the mythological role of the goddess in Yoruba traditions and also look at accounts of the experiences of women in contemporary cultural engagements of the traditions. Drawing from the work of Teresa N. Washington, bell hooks, Patricia Hill Collins, and Oyeronke Olajubu, this section applies black feminist thought to the analysis of power dynamics and gender issues surrounding practitioners. I conclude by highlighting prevalent themes and motifs and considering the role of "remembering, forgetting, and substituting" in the African American appropriation of Yoruba traditions. Shifting the focus from texts to worlds of experience and practice creates opportunities for greater understanding of the role of religious myth in shaping human consciousness and self-understanding.

My own fascination with "sacred performance" through the engagement of oral or written literature, myth, song, dance, sculpture, visual arts, ritual, rite, drama, or ceremony fuels this work. While I use ethnographic sources, *Divining the Self* is not a conventional ethnography. Rather, I use ethnography as a methodological tool for the study of diverse scripturalizing practices within a particular tradition. Using the archetypal journey motif, the study further focuses on the divinatory enterprise as key to the negotiation of selfhood and destiny.[44] The use of a performance paradigm as a point of departure positions "scriptures" as a site of production more than a site of interpretation, and it allows for a focus on "texts" beyond things written. This approach calls for an examination of the dynamic interaction involved in the production of "scripture," the phenomenon that Vincent Wimbush refers to as "signifying scriptures," that Victor Turner might call "social drama," and that Roland Barthes says is "governed by a metonymic rather than a hermeneutic logic."[45] This work, then, answers some questions as it generates others.

1

MYTHIC ORIGINS AND CULTURAL PRACTICES

The ancestral grounds on which the African American babalawo stands are scattered with debris, fragmented bones and broken shells, beads of glass, and beads of stone. But these grounds are not a desolate wasteland, nor a distant island, for they may be found in the midst of the hustle and bustle of the city and in the quiet tranquility of the countryside. Memories of the African ancestors saturate this landscape, extending to the other side of the waters where, in a previous life, those ancestors communicated with the divine and consulted the oracle. In the strange land to which they had been taken, the enslaved Africans turned to memories embedded deep in the soul, and they called forth the wisdom of the gods to make meaning of life.

Though the participants in my study had no memory of actual African kindred, they repeatedly referred to "ancestral memory." As Sheree Thomas observes,

> Since ancient times, oracles and diviners have combined their collected wisdom with close observation of the world. . . . Whether they chose to cast bones and shells, palm nuts gathered in gourd and calabash, read footprints in the dust, or rely upon a complex system of calculations rooted in sacred works such as *Path of Odu* or the *I Ching*, they drew upon cultural traditions handed down through

> generations. And these seemingly disparate practices of ancient cultures . . . shared one thing in common: the desire to change and impact the future.
>
> This desire to alter one's path, to understand how things have come to pass, is one of our most basic human impulses.[1]

The performative role of the Odu, the "scriptures" of the Yoruba, is but one example of this quest to understand the dynamic forces affecting one's life and to exercise agency in creating one's future. Here I use the term "scriptures" to refer to the active engagement of an oral corpus of material deemed to have a certain authority and relevance for assessing, interpreting, and shaping human behavior and activity. Generations removed from their places of origin and from these scriptural traditions, how is it that African Americans came to know, understand, embrace, and appropriate the Odu corpus and its accompanying ceremonial and ritual practices? I seek to construct a picture of ancient ancestral practices by examining contemporary accounts of ritual practices that were passed on from generation to generation through oral tradition in Nigeria. I then look at the practices of African American adherents for similarities. Finally, I connect orisha archetypes with elements of African American cultural history, suggesting that these archetypes were deeply embedded in African American cultural memory long before the Orisha tradition was formally embraced.

According to a senior priest of Ifa, for the Yoruba, "the odus are transmitters, transferring a spiritual energy into a physical world. The Odu is the universal and inhabited world experience in its most profound form. The odus are divinities, unchangeable, neither just nor logical. But the Odu might manifest through new and different life experiences, which at the root are spiritually the same, bringing about new *ese* Ifa, new verses, new stories that speak to the foundational spiritual experience."[2] The Odu as scripture is both text and performance—and referred to as both by the diviners with whom I spoke. Each odu is said to "fall" from heaven, and each may be described as "hot" or "cool." Each has a unique "signature," defining characteristics, distinctive attributes, and an infinite number of related stories and proverbs known as *ese*. In answer to my questions about the origin of the Odu, my informants relayed versions of several myths, which are reiterated in the work of Wande Abimbola.

This priest's claim that the odus are unchangeable is confusing and contradictory in light of other comments suggesting that the Odu is not a fixed text, but one in which the diviner and client mediate meaning unique to the personal situation at hand. The diviner's narrative is always different, reflecting the uniqueness of every situation. Is this claim to fixity an effort to validate the corpus in some way or is it a simple reference to the Odu as a basic index or indicator of a corpus of material relevant to a variety of life experiences? These questions warrant further consideration and investigation.

In *Ifá: An Exposition of Ifá Literary Corpus*, Abimbola writes that according to divination mythology, there was a time when there was not a barrier between heaven and earth. During this time it was possible to move freely between the two, and Ifa (also known as Orunmila) was one deity who did. According to Abimbola, some myths report that Ifa had "eight children and a number of disciples, all of whom he taught the secrets of divination" (5). Ifa was very wise and from time to time was called to heaven to help Olodumare (God) solve problems. After such a mission, Ifa would usually return to earth; however, on one occasion, after having been vexed by his children, he decided not to return. In Ifa's absence, earth fell into great disarray. Fertility cycles were interrupted. Life became nearly impossible. The people of the earth eventually went to the children of Ifa and asked them to go to heaven and beg their father to set things in order again. They did just that, but no amount of begging could convince Ifa to return to earth. He did, however, give each of his children sixteen palm nuts, and he instructed them on how to use them. The palm nuts would serve as a means of communicating with him, and the children would always be able to consult him about any problem or issue that might be of concern (5–7). Thus "the sixteen palm nuts known as *ikin* . . . have been used as an important part of the Ifá divination system from that time till today" (7).

Abimbola notes that there are other myths about the Odu and the Ifa divination system. One myth has it that before Orunmila's final return to heaven, he promised his children and his followers that he would send them certain divinities to perform some of the functions he performed while on earth. These divinities would be known as the Odu and would descend from heaven. They would govern all human affairs, and each one would cover certain areas. Orunmila's children and disciples waited and watched for the divinities to appear; as they appeared, they were assigned seniority based on the order of their appearance. The order of seniority became an important consideration in the interpretive process. The initial 16 divinities were called the parent Odu, the principals who gave birth to

240 others, who came to be known as the "Omo Odu" (the children of Odu). Each of the 256 odus is said to have an infinite number of *ese,* i.e., verses, stories, and proverbs that may be drawn upon by the diviner when consulting with a client (26–30). (The dynamics of such consultations and their effect on the client will be discussed in later chapters.)

Abimbola also cites two other popular myths about the origin of the Odu, one of which suggests that Ifa was once a very famous and very popular diviner known throughout Yorubaland for his skill. His fame was so great that hundreds of people begged him to accept them as disciples and apprentices; of those, he chose only sixteen men, and the names of these apprentices are identical to the sixteen divinatory signs called odus (7).[3] The other myth does not speak directly to the origin of the Odu but does suggest that the Ifa cult came about as the result of the skill of a famous diviner, Setilu. Setilu, blind from birth, was gifted with a second sight that allowed him to predict the future with great accuracy. He is said to have used sixteen small pebbles as his implements, and through his success and the success of the followers whom he initiated into the cult, Ifa gradually became the officially recognized "consulting oracle of the whole Yoruba nation" (8).[4] Another myth points to Oshun, the popular female orisha, as the original source of the Odu Ifa and suggests that the Ifa system of divination grew out of the sixteen-cowrie-shell, or *mirindilogun,* system, which was established by Oshun when she was the wife of Orunmila or Ifa. (For further discussion of this topic, see chapter 6.)

Yoruba Practices and African American Adaptations

According to Wande Abimbola, throughout history, the Yoruba people have organized their lives around Ifa: "Throughout the life of a person, Ifa is so important. From birth to death, a person goes to a diviner at every turn in his life. . . . The Yoruba have woven everything that is dear to them throughout the full range of their experience, from mythology to legends, to history and to contemporary times, around Ifa. In ancient times it was compulsory for every Yoruba person to have 'One Hand of Ifa'" (86). "One hand of Ifa" refers to the set of palm nuts that adherents receive as the formal entrance into the practice of their religion. The palm nuts, or *ikin,* are sometimes used by the diviner for divination and in general by practitioners when they consult the deity Orunmila, or Ifa, for guidance. (As noted above, Orunmila is the god of divination, while Ifa may refer to the same deity or to the religion itself.) Through the *ikin*, the "hermeneutics of power" becomes visible.

As anthropologist Andrew Apter notes, the sixteen major divisions of the Odu are named for the sixteen "original" Yoruba kingdoms and the sixteen apprentices selected from the kingdoms.[5] Apter, drawing from the work of William Bascom as well as Ulli Beier, suggests that each odu gives a true but coded account of past events. In his words, the form and content of the odus not only give order to Yoruba myths and establish the relationship between the deities but also establish relationships between kingdoms.[6] His emphasis on the politics of power and the channeling of power through political kingdoms highlights political dynamics at an institutional level rather than that of individual participants. According to several practitioners, the orisha "speak" through the odus, and every odu has a physical relationship to the body. Awo Fá'lokun Fatunmbi lists the correlation between the odus and the various parts of the body as shown in figure 3.[7]

As Fatunmbi explains it, "The type of ashe [energy/power] that is drawn to each location is affected by the *Odu* that controls a particular part of the body. . . . but each *Odu* represents a primal form of energy with its own unique characteristics."[8] This fundamental principle of energy correlation is a reflection of the embodied and performative nature of the Odu. The divination ritual is a "reading" of how particular energies, expressed as certain odus, are "performing" in the life of an individual at a given point in time. The diviner/practitioner then frequently consults the oracle for a reading on what energies are at work and with what likely consequences. In providing corrective prescriptions, the diviner takes these energy scans into consideration.

Yoruba-derived divination practices in North America vary, but ancestral reverence is a common thread. As part of the invocation prayers preceding each session, diviners recite the ancestral lineage of their ritual family. In consulting the oracle on behalf of a client, they also identify the individual by referring to the client's name, date of birth, and mother's name. In other rituals related to birth readings and initiations, participants are expected to recite the names of maternal and paternal ancestors from several generations. Every practitioner maintains some form of ancestral altar, and divination may serve as a means of ancestral communication. One's ancestors, also referred to as the *egun*, may speak through the Odu.[9]

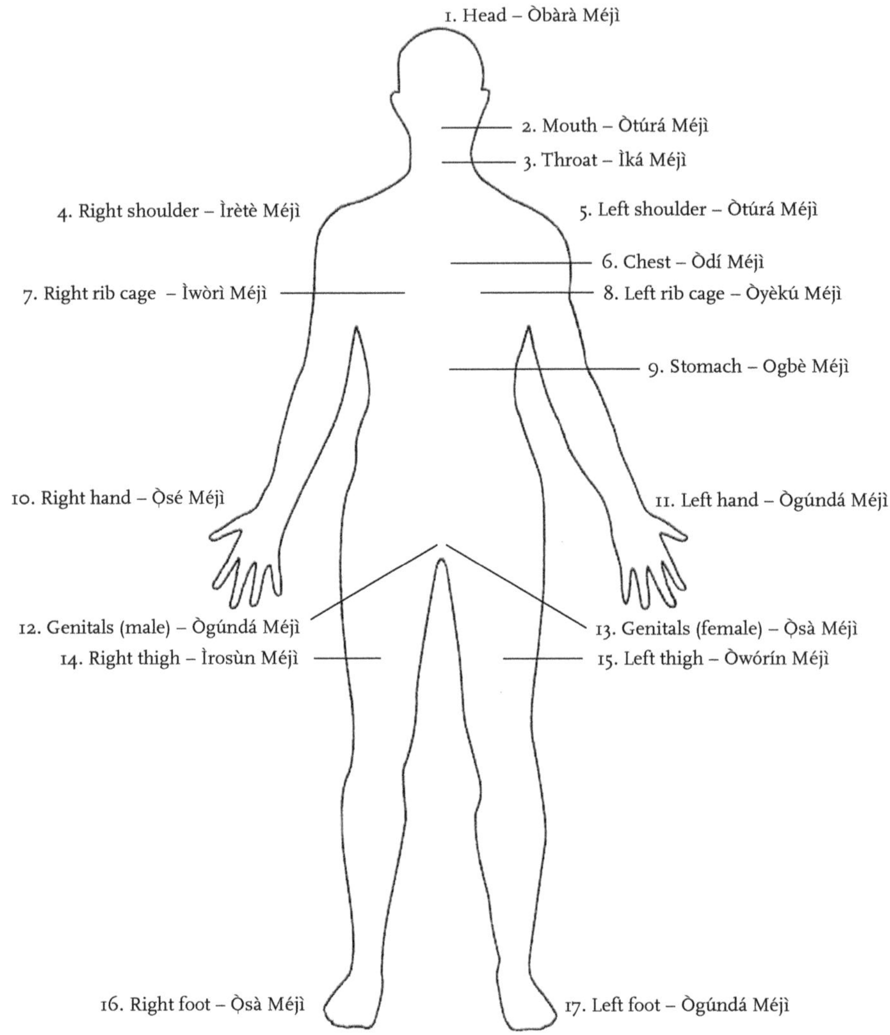

Figure 3 Correlations between the odus and parts of the body

Odu and the Birth Reading

Among the Yoruba, the birth reading is a common practice and is, in the traditional culture, an individual's first encounter with the Odu. Called "stepping into the world," the birth reading provides a kind of road map for the parents of the infant. It indicates from which ancestral lineage the child has come, what orisha is protecting the child, and the purpose for which the child has come into the world. It also identifies the child's taboos, of which the parents should be aware; what personality traits the child is likely to exhibit; and what challenges the child is likely to face.[10] African American practitioners have also adopted and adapted this practice, as I witnessed in Atlanta, Georgia.

Birth Reading in Atlanta

"She comes into the world to bring joy. Oshun is protecting her." The diviner, a babalawo from Oyotunji Village, sat at the kitchen table of a young African American couple in an upscale suburb of Atlanta. Wearing traditional attire in a green and tan print, he had come with his beaded diviner's bag at the request of the young mother. She was not a Yoruba practitioner but nevertheless had asked for a "birth reading" for her newborn daughter. I joined them at the table and watched intently as the diviner touched the infant and cast his chain, marking the odu in a spiral-bound notebook that he pulled from his diviner's bag. He continued his narrative:

> She is a blessing that comes to you as a result of reacquainting yourself with the traditional ways. This blessing comes from the venerated ancestors in Heaven. You will have a lot of resources available to you as you raise this child. She may have a tendency to always want things to be pleasant and peaceful and as a result will not want to accept responsibility for anything that goes wrong. You will have to teach her at an early age to accept responsibility for her actions. You have to teach her to have a strong sense of ethics and self-respect. She comes with some spirit friends. They are wonderful little angels now, but you don't want them to turn into the dirty diaper gang, so periodically, about once a month you need to clean her aura. Just take a piece of fruit and go over her body with it. Then discard the fruit. Throw it out there by the tree [he gestured toward the backyard]. She comes from her mother's ancestral line. Her name . . . in Yoruba culture, names are given to reflect the circumstances under which a child is born. She is the first-born daughter, so one name would be Asabi [pronounced "A-sha-bee"], a second name would be Modupe [pronounced "Mo-do-pay"], meaning thanks. When you get frustrated with her, remember how much you wanted a child and by calling her name, Modupe, you are expressing your thankfulness.

The young mother laughed and prepared to take the baby, who by this time had fallen asleep, upstairs for a nap. The diviner encouraged her to plan a formal naming ceremony and "stepping into the world" ritual in the presence of other members of the family.[11]

The birth reading reflects one significant point in time in which the oracle is consulted for guidance and insight into one's life. This scene in Atlanta is in many respects very similar to a birth reading in contemporary Nigeria described by Margaret Thompson Drewal in *Yoruba Ritual.* As Drewal points out in her discussion of ritual and "new beginnings," the birth reading marks the child's entry point on the road of life, officially known as "stepping into the world." In Nigeria, this ritual of "new beginnings" is customarily followed by a second ritual a few months later, called "knowing the head." It is performed to identify the nature of the child's "inner head" (*inu ori*), i.e., the personality traits with which the child was born (56). The divination narrative issued as a result of the birth reading serves as a resource for parents, a set of personal "scriptures" to draw from in raising the child. This practice reflects the Yoruba orientation to the world: life is seen as a never-ending cyclical journey, birth being one point of passage. Every important passage is accompanied by divination to assess one's progress along the journey (56).

Odu and Initiation

Another "rite of passage" in which the diviner/priest offers a set of "scriptures" that provide what Drewal calls "models for self-examination and self-interpretation" is the initiation ceremony, known as Itefa in traditional Yoruba practice and as Ocha among Lucumi orisha worshippers in America (63). The traditional diviners conceptualize the fourteen-day Itefa ritual "as a journey with travel from one place to another, and a return; new experiences; joys and hardships along the route; and material for further contemplation and reflection" (ibid.). This journey to the sacred grove, the *igbodou,* is designed especially for six- to seven-year-old boys whose lives have not yet been formed, as well as for adult males whose lives have been broken and scattered. This rite of passage is marked by a period of physical separation from family and friends. During this time, the initiate is accompanied by only the diviners and other initiated students. Elaborate rituals and ceremonies precede the entrance into the sacred grove. Through such ceremonies, the diviners build up the energy of the palm nuts that they will later give to the initiate, invoke the blessings of the spirits, and request permission to enter the sacred space. The journey home is just as elaborate (63–65). Describing the Itefa rituals and ceremonies she observed in Nigeria, Drewal writes,

> On the inside of the grove, initiates experience many "wonders" that were kept secret from the uninitiated. Part of the importance of making a portion of the journey secret was to preserve the intensity and impact of experiencing it for the first time. During the period of separation, males were given rebirth. In the wee hours of the morning as the sun rose, the initiate and his family learned through divination the set of texts that "brought him to the world," that defined his personality and potential in life. . . .
>
> By the evening of the second day, the initiates emerged from the grove with heads shaved and painted white, wearing white cloth and the red tail feather of the African grey parrot on their foreheads. . . . The white cloth is the color of the birth caul, and thus the color worn by all human beings when coming into the world anew. In painting the initiate's head with "star chalk" . . . the diviners made a visual analogy between the newly defined personality of the individual and a shining star.
>
> The group journeyed home again as elaborately as it had journeyed to the *igbodu*. Once back in Ọṣitọla's house the initiates were confined to specially prepared mats (*itẹn*), where they slept and ate for the next twelve days. There, too, all the subsequent divinations were performed.
>
> On the third day (*ita* Ifa), the diviners checked their progress through divination. . . . the greater part of the day was taken for feasting, dancing, and playing. Between the third and seventh days, the initiates formally saluted the deities first thing every morning, rested, and ate. On the seventh day . . . they again made sacrifices, feasted, and danced. The fourteenth day . . . the novices were reincorporated into their ordinary daily routine. (66–72)

The new initiates return to their daily routines with a set of personal "scriptures" to study, reflect upon, and contemplate. The quest is to understand one's relationship to these "scriptures" at any given point in time. The interpretive process never ends (77). Present-day orisha initiation ceremonies in the Lucumi system as practiced in New York City are strikingly similar to the one described by Drewal, as I observed.

Ocha Ceremony in Harlem

The *igbodou* was a small corner of a room on the ground level of a Harlem brownstone on Striver's Row, a tree-lined street known for its upscale clientele. This corner of the room, draped in golden yellow fabrics, was designated "the throne" and would serve as the "home" of the initiate for seven days. On the floor, in this one corner of the room, on a straw mat covered with a white sheet, he would sleep, eat, and sit. The sponsoring priest, referred to as the initiate's "godfather," and the *ajubona*, the second godfather, would assume responsibility for the initiation and follow-up training. They had assembled a crew of about fifteen initiated priests and priestesses, all of whom would be key players in this elaborate production. An air of expectancy filled the place as the crew prepared for the official beginning of the initiation ceremonies. With few exceptions, they all wore white.

The entrance to the *igbodou* was covered with a white sheet. Only initiated priests were allowed to enter. From my post in the kitchen, I could hear prayers, chants, and songs along with animal sounds coming from the closed doors of the *igbodou*. The senior priests who were not working sat on the patio just off the kitchen and kept a lively conversation going about the religion, people in the religion, the past, the future, the present. The smell of wet feathers, blood, spices, herbs, and cigar smoke permeated the air.

After about six hours of private ceremony and ritual, the oriate, or ritual leader, emerged and raised the curtain. When I went in I saw that the young initiate's head had been shaved and painted white. He was smiling and appeared relaxed and refreshed. Having seen his weary state a few hours earlier, I couldn't imagine how this change had come about. In the terminology of the practitioners, the young man had been "made." He had been "crowned." The *ashe* of his guardian orisha had been placed in his head. The next day would be his "throne" day, a festive occasion of drumming, dancing, and fellowship in celebration of his new status, the beginning of his *yawo* year, or first year as a new initiate in the Yoruba priesthood.

The celebration began at 2:00 P.M. The *yawo* was dressed in a rich gold color and wore a sparkling crown. The guests gathered, bringing flowers and cash as congratulatory gifts for the "baby priest." As the ceremony opened, he stood between his godfather and *ajubona* for the ceremonial playing of the drums. About fifty friends and supporters gathered around and watched approvingly. As the drummers broke into lively celebratory rhythms, the crowd spilled into the street, and curious passersby stopped to listen to the captivating beat. After a few hours, the guests shared a Cuban-style home-cooked meal and began to depart. The drummers played a closing rhythm while a middle-aged woman danced gracefully about the room and out the door with a bucket of water, which she threw into the street. This closing ritual represented a cleansing of the energy in the room. Several senior priests lingered for conversation with the "baby priest," and finally his godfather announced that the "baby" needed his rest. The following day I arrived at 8:30 A.M. for the ita reading. The oriate, the godfather, the *ajubona*, and several other priests who had assisted during the ceremonies of the past few days were present. The ita reading began with a cast for the *yawo*'s new name. After a brief discussion of the meaning of the name, the oriate proceeded with the reading, casting the shells from each orisha's plate, announcing the odu, its orientation, and his interpretation. As part of the consultation with the oracle of each orisha, the oriate also inquired about any *ebo* (sacrifice) required. The recorder wrote this information in the *yawo*'s ita journal. It would become his personal set of "scriptures," but would be kept by his godfather until the end of his first year.[12]

The divination narratives, known as the ita, from the initiation ceremonies as well as the birth reading described above are about an understanding of the self. The birth ita produces an initial set of personal "scriptures" from which the parents of an infant may draw insights to help understand the new life they are responsible for guiding. The initiation ita parallels the birth ita: it is also about understanding the self, but on a deeper level, in a different rite of passage. It is intended to provide another personal set of scriptures from which the "godparents" may draw insights as they seek to guide the new initiate into a greater understanding of the self in relationship to the world. Both may be seen as "scripturalizing practices," and as such, they reflect what Elizabeth Baeten refers to as "myth's abiding power."[13]

In Yoruba philosophy, every individual is said to embody a primary odu, representing a specific energy pattern. Every orisha, as a force of nature, also embodies a primary odu; consequently, every individual is linked to a specific orisha through the associated energy matrix of a particular odu. The individual, then, is initiated to the orisha with whom she or he has an energy affinity.[14] But as all orisha are considered to be forces of nature as well as aspects of the self, the practitioner strives to live in harmony with nature and in harmony with the self. The divination narrative, with its prescriptive ebo, or sacrifice, is one of the means for establishing and maintaining balance.

Odu and Ebo

According to Wande Abimbola, every complete divination process carries with it a prescribed sacrifice. The Yoruba priest/diviner is responsible for knowing what ebo is associated with every odu, and after giving the divination narrative, the priest informs the client of the prescribed sacrifice, which may include various raw or cooked foods, live animals, fowls, plants, or stones. Ifa and Orisha priests maintain that sacrifice is very important and helps "unite all of the forces, both natural and supernatural, that operate in Yoruba society."[15] J. Omosade Awolalu, scholar of religion at the University of Ibadan, identifies two categories of sacrifice in the traditional culture: those intended to provide feasts for the supernatural beings and community of worshippers, and those intended to avert calamity. He further divides these categories as follows: thanksgiving, votive, propitiatory, preventive, substitutionary, and foundational.[16]

As Awolalu explains in *Yoruba Beliefs and Sacrificial Rites*, thanksgiving and communion sacrifices provide an opportunity for practitioners to share a common meal with the supernatural powers or divinities to whom they wish to offer thanks for the preservation of life and for success in particular endeavors. As an example, Awolalu cites the annual yam festival, in which farmers gather yams from the first new crop and ceremonially present them to the divinities, spirits, and ancestors as an expression of thanks for fertile soil and sustenance. This elaborate festival includes much singing, dancing, and praying as all members of the community join the *oba* (king) and the chief priests in offering prayers for blessings in the coming year (146–49). The votive sacrifice is another form of thanksgiving. During festivals for the divinities, devotees appear with offerings to fulfill the vows they made during previous festivals. For instance, at the annual Olua festival, devotees kneel and petition the gods for certain things, promising an offering in return for the fulfillment of their requests: "Invariably, year after year, men and women come to fulfill their vows bringing such items as fowls, goats, kola-nuts, pigeons, salt and other items" (151). Such actions are based on the belief that the "law of exchange" governs the universe, i.e., receiving requires giving. Ritual sacrifice, therefore, appears to be an embodied expression of this principle.

The propitiatory sacrifice, on the other hand, is called for when the oracle reveals that an individual or community has offended the spirits that control some aspect of human affairs. Such sacrifices may include animals, fowls, or valuable objects but are not accompanied by communal feasts. The propitiatory sacrifice is, instead, a solemn occasion in which adherents chase away "evil spirits" or negative energies that are preventing the experience of balance and harmony in daily life. In many instances, purification rites are performed along with the propitiatory sacrifice. The purification rite is for the general spiritual cleansing of the community. In such rites, at noon on the appointed day, the adults of each household smudge every corner of the house with a smoking torch and then carry the torch into the streets and from there to the bush and to a flowing stream. Following this ritual, sacrifices for peace and calm are offered to the designated deity (152–56).

If sacrifice can remove malevolent spirits from the life of the individual or the community, then sacrifice also can prevent the misfortunes that could result from the activity of such forces. When the oracle reveals potential danger ahead, the diviner prescribes a preventive or substitutionary ebo. While both are performed to avoid some calamity or undesirable experience, the substitutionary ebo offers an animal to the spirits in the place of the person who should have suffered the discomfort, misfortune, or death.

Awolalu's survey of sacrificial rites lists the "foundational sacrifice" as the final category, the one that may contain all of the elements identified above. The foundational sacrifice is based on the principle that every new undertaking, in order to be successful, must be blessed by the gods. The diviner, therefore, consults the oracle to determine what forces are surrounding this new venture and what ebos are necessary for success. As a clear illustration of this principle, Awolalu cites the following example:

> If, for example, a Yorùbá man wants to build a house, he normally finds out by means of oracle if the proposed site is safe for human habitation. If there is any bad spirit dwelling on the spot, it is propitiated by means of sacrifice. At the same time, once the anger of the spirit has been assuaged, it is expected that there will be no further cause for anxiety. In other words, future calamity is prevented in consequence of the propitiatory sacrifice offered. But when the building

> has been completed, there is also the so-called "house-warming" ceremony when friends, families and admirers come to rejoice with the owner of the house. This is an occasion for joy and thanksgiving. (160)

Similar African American practices include divination and prescribed ebos for new ventures. Initiates divine to determine where their "orisha pots," altars, and religious symbols should be placed in a new residence. The above example illustrates the extent to which sacrifice is a critical aspect of orisha worship. It also points to how the Odu performs in the lives of the people, for the ritual sacrifices are prescribed through the diviner's interpretation of each odu and its associated ebo. In every instance, the sacrifice is an effort to influence the forces that affect human affairs, thereby exerting power and agency in shaping one's experience of the world.

Among African American Ifa diviners, not all divination readings prescribe an ebo, though every odu has an associated ebo. It often depends upon the "orientation" of the reading, i.e., whether it is connected with *ire* (positive energies) or *ogsobo* (negative energies). However, sacrifice always forms an integral part of certain events. For example, all major initiations include foundational ebos for new beginnings.[17] As Oba Oseijeman Adefunmi I, founder of Oyotunji Village, explains it, certain ebos are necessary for an individual to be "made," a term used to refer to the initiation process. Adefunmi suggests that the blood of the animals and fowls drained into orisha pots over certain herbs, rocks, and minerals produce a subtle chemical reaction and emit certain vibrating, living energies akin to the astral energies produced by planets. The orisha pots thus "represent a connection to the universe."[18]

Traditionally, sacrifice is part of the annual Odun festivals organized around each orisha. Drawing from this ancient tradition, the priesthood of Oyotunji Village conducts orisha festivals on assigned dates in relationship to the planetary energies with which each orisha is said to be most closely aligned. The major orisha, corresponding planetary influences, month of celebration, and associated odus are listed in the table opposite.[19]

The events are very similar to those described in the literature on ancient Yorubaland. These religious celebrations include various rituals and ceremonies, including purification rites, sacrifice, divination, mythic dramatizations, processions, singing, chanting, drumming, and dancing. These annual observances in honor of the orisha are practiced by adherents throughout the African Diaspora. During the course of my research,

Date	Festival	Planetary influence	Odu
January	Reading of the Year		
February	Olokun (deity of the deep sea)	Neptune	Irosun
March	Esu, Ogun, Oshosi, Men's Akinkonju Festival (trickster, war, and hunter deities; rites of passage for men)	Mercury, Mars, Sagittarius	Okanran, Ogunda, Oworin
April–May	Oshun (deity of love and spring)	Venus	Oshe
May–June	Egungun (celebration of the ancestors)		
June	Yemonja (rites of passage for women)	Moon	Odi
July	Ifa Festival and Yoruba National Convention	Sun	
July	Shango Festival (deity of thunder and lightning)	Uranus	Obara
August	Obatala Festival (patron deity of Oyotunji Village)	Jupiter	Ejionle
October	Oya Festival (deity of death)	Pluto	Osa
October	Hwedo Festival (honoring the unknown dead)		
December	Babaluaiye (winter solstice and taskmaster)	Saturn	

I observed such festivals in New York and South Carolina. The festivals serve as a kind of reunion for practitioners, attracting adherents throughout the United States.[20]

The Cuban Link

How did African Americans come to embrace the Odu literary corpus and related ritual practices? Without exception, the people with whom I consulted agreed that a variation of the system was preserved in Cuba and became accessible to African Americans when large numbers of Cubans migrated to the United States in the late 1950s. Ócha'ni Lele, himself a practitioner and initiated priest, has recorded the myth/history as it was told to him. As Lele relates the story in *The Diloggún*, "before humans knew of orishas or odu, there was only Orúnmila. Born from Olódumare [God] herself, Orúnmila was the great witness to creation and knew all things. He incarnated among mortals, bringing his infinite knowledge of odu and divination to earth. Orúnmila's teachings are known as *Ifá*."[21] Beginning with one babalawo, Lele continues, the cult spread throughout Yorubaland, "and from it the original sixteen-cowrie-shell oracle evolved" (ibid.).

Lele further explains that it was through the Africans enslaved in Cuba that a broken and fragmented knowledge of the Odu and the sixteen-cowrie-shell system of divination began to grow in the New World. Through the forced immigration of large numbers of Africans (many of whom were Yoruba) over an extended period of time—349 years, according to Lele—a continual stream of knowledge related to orisha worship flowed from the homeland to enslaved Africans in Cuba: "Of all the New World territories involved in slave importation, Cuba boasted the longest history. While slaves were imported to Brazil in 1538 and to the colonies of North America in 1619, in Cuba they arrived as early as 1521. . . . Cubans held on to the slavery system the longest; not until 1870, twenty years after the abolition of slavery in Brazil and ten years after abolition in the United States, did slavery come to an end in Cuba" (2).

But it was not the length of time that the slave trade existed, nor the number of Yoruba among the enslaved Africans, that alone accounted for the survival of the traditional religion. A major contributing factor was the royal decree, signed by the king of Spain in 1789, declaring that all slave owners were to teach their slaves the religion of the Roman Catholic Church. Lele notes that the implementation of this decree, "The Royal Document on the Trades and Occupations of Slaves," ultimately created space for the survival of traditional African religion not only in Cuba but in America as well (4).[22]

In keeping with the guidelines of the Royal Document, the *cofradia* or the *cabildo*, an organization that had proven to be very successful in the enculturation of new Catholic converts in Spain, was established for the religious instruction of the enslaved Africans in Cuba. *Cofradia* leaders were appointed from the ranks of the most respected and most devout among them. These individuals, who came to be known as "godparents," openly taught their groups about the worship of the Catholic saints; secretly, they taught them about the African myths and spirits. "Very quickly," Lele explains, "the various ethnic groups brought together in a cofradia saw that all their spirits were related . . . and that they could, in secret, hide the worship of their spirits behind the guise of the saints" (4).

Legend has it that practitioners took the statues of the Catholic saints, hollowed out space on the inside to conceal the orisha implements, and then resealed the bottom of the statues. Having done this, they could appear to be praying to and worshiping the saints, and all the while they were praying to and worshiping their own deities. Their oppressors thought it odd that the slaves were so attached to the saints, and thus the name Santeria (the way of the saints) was assigned to this peculiar style of worship.[23]

In *The Diloggún*, Lele attributes the codification of the Cuban system of Lucumi to the diligence of four members of the priesthood who rose to prominence during the late 1800s and early 1900s: Mama Monserrate (Obatero), Octavio Sama (Obadimelli), Timotea Albear (Ayai La Tuan), and Ferminita Gomez (Ochabi). They were responsible for fashioning and passing on what later became known as the Lucumi system. Little is known of Mama Monserrate, except that she was held in high esteem and that under her leadership, Cuban practitioners began to establish the Lucumi system of the Yoruba religion. Two of the many she initiated into the religion became well known: Octavio Sama, known as Obadimelli, and Ferminita Gomez, known as Ochabi (10).

According to the story passed down, Octavio was studying to be a priest of Ifa in Nigeria but was never initiated, because while he was a child, he and his mother were captured and taken to Cuba as slaves. However, once he was in Cuba, Mama Monserrate recognized his potential and initiated him into the Lucumi faith. Based on his knowledge of Ifa, Octavio established the sixteen-cowrie-shell system of divination. But, Lele notes, it was through his work with a Nigerian priestess of Shango, Timotea Albear, the first female oriate of the Lucumi tradition, that the system was codified (11).

Ferminita Gomez, another influential godchild of Mama Monserrate, was considered one of the most powerful practitioners in the early 1900s. According to Lele, her most important contribution to the widespread practice of the religion was her detailed documentation of the ritual practices, her "clearly written libretas." Gomez is also credited with establishing the practice of giving several orisha when an initiate is crowned, rather than only the one that "rules the head." This practice was established to ensure the survival and continuation of the religion in a hostile environment (ibid.).

In his historical treatment of Santeria in the United States, anthropologist George Brandon identifies the period between 1959 and 1982 as one in which thousands of Cubans migrated to major urban areas in the United States, including New York City. They entered during a time of grave political, social, and cultural upheaval, reflected in the civil rights, Black Power, and women's rights movements. It was difficult for newcomers to gain footing in a culture that was itself in the midst of change. Through Santeria, many Cuban immigrants found a source of help in making meaning out of their new lives and negotiating the social circumstances in which they now found themselves.[24]

It was also during this time that Walter Eugene King, later to become Oba Oseijeman Adefunmi I, was initiated in Cuba and returned to New York City as a strong advocate of black cultural nationalism. This political ideology, interacting with an African religious tradition of empowerment, found fertile ground in African American communities. The history of African American engagement of the Odu Ifa is generally traced to or from this point.[25] However, I suggest, as I did at the beginning of this chapter, that a land covered with fragmented bones and broken shells might serve as a metaphor for the variety of ways in which the metaphysical principles underlying the traditions associated with the Odu Ifa have historically been expressed by African Americans. Marta Vega, a scholar/practitioner and founder of the Caribbean Cultural Center/African Diaspora Institute in New York City, identified one way when she wrote of Esu/Elegba as the mythological figure that stands at the crossroads, connecting the mundane visible world of *aye* with the invisible spirit world of *orun*. As she points out, the trickster figure is often referred to as demonic, but she offers a corrective to such readings, focusing on the metaphysical aspects and social functions of the trickster:

> This trickster and divine messenger is an orisá who reflects the contradictions that humans must resolve in order to live a balanced, healthy, and prosperous life. . . . In a nation of contradiction, the divine messenger and trickster can turn everything upside down and still survive at the juncture between the spirit world and the visible world. This is the sacred space that Africans in the Diaspora have occupied in order to resist and survive enslavement and its aftermath. It is also the space that has provided them the authority to re-create a unique, New World version of the sacred African aesthetic vision.[26]

Perhaps this space that Marta Vega describes is not unlike that recognized by W. E. B. Du Bois when he wrote, "One ever feels his twoness,—an American, a Negro; two souls, two thoughts, two unreconciled strivings; two warring ideals in one dark body, whose dogged strength alone keeps it from being torn asunder."[27] Vega's depiction of African Americans as living in a nation of contradictions, seeking meaning at a juncture between the spirit world and the visible world, reflects the Esu principle of duality. Both Vega and Du Bois suggest that African Americans lived the principle of duality long before Oba Oseijeman received the one hand of Ifa and formally embraced orisha worship. They expressed this duality in their spirituals, their sorrow songs, their freedom songs, their blues, their fictions, their poetry, and their sermons. Drawing from the Esu/Elegba energy as well as other orisha archetypes, they reframed their experiences, rewrote the narrative, retold the story, and reinvented and resituated the self.

Dance, Drumming, and Chanting

In her discussion of dance in ancient Yorubaland, Ọmọ́fọláḅọ̀ S. Àjàyí notes that dance is a microcosm of the culture, serving as a system of nonverbal communication that conveys significant themes in the context of the sacred festival. Grounding her work in semiotic theory, she discusses the "body sign" as signification and communication, in both the production and the exchange of meanings. Drawing examples from the Obatala Festival and the Shango Festival in Yorubaland, Àjàyí explains how unique movements of the body in space portray the essence of each of the deities and communicate the concepts associated with each.[28] The mythology surrounding each orisha serves as the springboard, or "text," from which festival activities, including song, symbol, and dance, draw their inspiration.

For example, the low, stooped posture and slow movements of the Obatala dance communicate the patience, humility, coolness, and peacefulness for which this deity stands. Àjàyí writes, "The dignified coolness of the Ọbàtálá Dance can be related to the snail, an important iconic symbol in the òrìsa-Nla [another name for Obatala, the great orisha] concept. The sacred animal of Ọbàtálá, the snail is naturally a 'cool,' wet, slow animal."[29] By contrast, the hot-natured Shango is danced with a furious energy and fast, thrusting movements. Like his iconic symbol, the double-edged ax, Shango's dance has sharp edges depicted through jerky shoulder movements. The Shango dancer in costume wears a skirt that twirls about like flames of fire. In Àjàyí's words, "The dynamic, restless energy perceived in Ṣàngó's Dance signifies the totality of his unbridled passion, fury, and irrationality . . . like the flash of lightning darting nervously across the sky."[30]

These two examples illustrate the significance of dance as a form of religious communication in orisha worship. Every orisha has unique dance movements that reflect its attributes, and, by the same token, there is an implicit relationship with the Odu, for each orisha is said to "own" certain odus. When practitioners dance in honor of their guardian orisha, they are also reflecting and expressing the "energies" most prevalent in their psychic composition.

Where there is dancing, there is drumming. The drums play a significant role in religious communication among the Yoruba, and just as every orisha has characteristic dance steps, so every orisha has characteristic drumbeats, tempos, and rhythms.[31] The drum in Africa has long been recognized as an instrument of liturgy and mediation with the sacred. During the colonial period, Christian missionaries and colonial administrators confiscated and destroyed thousands of drums, for they perceived the drum as "satanic."[32] In his interview with Wande Abimbola about *bata*, *dundun*, and drum literature, Ivor Miller noted that Cuba is the only country in the Americas that has been able to maintain a continuous *bata* tradition.[33] When questioned by Miller, Abimbola confirmed that the names of famous Cuban *bata* drummers were in fact African names. The following interview excerpt further explains the traditional use of the drum in Yorubaland and its survival in Cuba.

Ivor: How would you evaluate the difference between *bàtá* playing in Cuba and Nigeria?

Wande: There is a lot of correspondence between the language of Cuban *bàtá*, the rhythm, the melodies, and *bàtá* as played in Africa. There are also significant differences: the Cuban *bàtá* ensemble is made of three drums—our own ensemble is made of five drums. In Africa the *bàtá* has a living literature. Trained musicians can render songs and chants from the literature of *bàtá*, and they can also use *bàtá* to imitate ordinary speech, they can almost talk to somebody with it. But in Cuba, a good part of the literature has been forgotten. . . .

Ivor: . . . What do you mean specifically when you say a drum can speak?

Wande: When we say a drum "speaks" we are referring to the literature of that drum that the drummer has learned by heart, and which his audience also knows by heart. . . .

Ivor: Ever since *bàtá* drums were recreated in Cuba, they have been used to play for specific ceremonies vital to the continuity of the Lukumí religion. . . . *Bàtá* is played to witness the "birth" of a new priest, as well as their death. . . . How are *bàtá* used in Yorubaland?

Wande: *Bàtá* is a very versatile drum. If you are naming a baby, you can call a *bàtá* drummer. If you are installing a chief, the *bàtá* drummers will come. In Nigeria, *bàtá* is used for Egúngún, for Ṣàngó, Ògún, and for all social and religious occasions as well.[34]

In contemporary incarnations of Yoruba traditions, the drum continues its significance. The drums are ceremoniously consecrated and drummers have their "hands washed," i.e., they are initiated into a society of drummers. The rhythm of the drum and the devotees' response lead to possession, and a devotee in possession is a "voice of the gods," just as the odu is.[35] Adherents have commented that the drum is important because it "calls down the orisha." But the power of sound is not restricted to the vibrations of the drum and other musical instruments; it also resides in the human voice. Every babalawo in the ancient tradition recites *ese* Ifa (verses) aloud every morning. When the babalawo or *iyanifa* (a female Ifa initiate) divines, he or she chants verses from the odu that falls. In traditional practice, chanting the odu is considered an integral and important aspect of divining. Aside from the opening prayers, chanting is not a consistent part of New World divination practices, but it is a significant part of initiations and other celebratory occasions. The power of sound is also an important aspect of the role the odu performs in herbology:

> People who practice Yorùbá medicine, including Yorùbá Muslims and Christians, make use of Odù Ifá in their medicine. They print the Odù on the medicine and recite some incantations related to that Odù on the medicine to make it efficacious. That aspect is very important. Most of the medicines that the *babaláwo* make are connected to Ifá. Every *ẹsẹ* Ifá has three layers. One is the literary utterances themselves. Two is the *ògùn*, or leaves, herbs, roots that can be used to make a medicine which usually emanate from the verses as well. The third part is a talisman which is prepared through certain utterances related to that particular verse. . . . an accomplished *babaláwo* must know these three aspects.[36]

Certain plants are related to each orisha and each odu. For instance, there are the sixteen "leaves of Ifá and the seven plants of Ògún."[37] The enslaved Africans in America, coming from a variety of ethnic groups, all held extensive knowledge of herbal medicines. One book is often cited as witness to this knowledge: *The Narrative of the Life and Adventures of Henry Bibb, an American Slave*, published in 1849.[38] From Bibb's narrative, historians of African American religions have gleaned that

> many slaves put their confidence not in pro-slavery preaching but in an alternative system of belief variously known as conjure, hoodooing, or root doctoring. The practitioners used various charms and concoctions to inflict misfortune, tell the future, protect their clients, and . . . aid in affairs of the heart. . . . The practices of herbalism, divination, and conjuration survived alongside Christianity in the folk culture of southern blacks . . . long after the Civil War. Conjuration served as a countercultural protest to the worldview of the dominant society and met needs in the slave quarters that Christianity did not.[39]

According to the comments of several practitioners in South Carolina as well as New York, these practices have survived alongside Christianity even to the present day. A babalawo in South Carolina reports,

> When we first started the village, people were curious as to what we were doing, but after a while they started coming for services. Some people would come at night after dark, but others were bolder. They would come on Sunday afternoon still dressed up in their church clothes. Diviners used to get more business on Sunday than any other time, but now people come all during the week as well. Now people have jobs where they can take off during the week. There were a couple of famous "root doctors" in the area. Recently, one elderly lady died and they had a memorial service for her in the church. I was a friend of hers and they asked me to come and give remarks. While I was giving my talk I looked out at the audience and I saw a lot of people who were my clients. They were her clients too, but they were all active in the church. That was kind of funny to me.[40]

A priestess in New York makes similar comments: "A large percentage of orisha worshippers in America are Christian . . . Baptist. They'll tell you 'I have to go to church.' I would go myself sometime for I like the singing and the fellowship, but I don't want people to think the orisha can't take care of me. . . . A lot of Christians don't wear *elekes* [beaded necklaces indicating the first level of initiation into the practice of the Orisha tradition] but they have them. It's like what they say about the numbers, 'everybody hitting but nobody playing.'"[41]

These comments were underscored by the fact that I met and interviewed this priestess while attending the Blue Nile Rites of Passage culminating ceremony at one of New York's largest and most prestigious Baptist churches, Abyssinian Baptist Church. Founded in 1808 and taking its name from Abyssinia, or Ethiopia, the birthplace of several of its founding members, the church was established when a group of African Americans and Ethiopians decided that they would no longer tolerate the discriminatory practices of the First Baptist Church of New York City.[42] Several Orisha practitioners serve as consultants to Abyssinia's Blue Nile Rites of Passage program on an annual basis. They offer workshops on African and African American history during the yearlong training program and help design the rituals for the culminating event. These individuals coordinate rites of passage programs within the Orisha community and incorporate many of the same elements in the church programs.[43] Similar programs are conducted by the Yemonja Egbe of Brooklyn, New York.[44]

2

ORISHA ARCHETYPES, CULTURAL MEMORY, AND THE ODU

In his discussion of how societies remember, Paul Connerton argues that "images and recollected knowledge of the past are conveyed and sustained by (more or less) ritual performances" and that these are bodily performances.[1] Carl Jung argues for the existence of an inherited collective unconscious through which archetypal forms are given expression.[2] Arthur Flowers, an African American novelist and poet, speaks of the "tribal soul" as the "consciousness of a people. Its group psyche. Its way. . . . The soul of a people as shaped and reflected in their culture and their literature."[3] Through the lens of these concepts I examine selected forms of African American musical expression as historical "texts" reflecting certain archetypal representations of the "Orisha energy matrix" associated with the Yoruba pantheon and embedded in the collective unconscious of African American people. Through a brief look at spirituals and the blues, I point out how these musical expressions serve as reservoirs of meaning and systems of communication.

Spirituals, the Blues, and Esu

Sung by African Americans since the earliest days of slavery, spirituals served as a kind of psychic release or escape from the harshness and cruelty of everyday life: "Certainly, 'this world is not my home' was a steady theme in the spirituals, one that offered its singers/hearers visions of a peaceful, loving realm beyond the one in which they labored."[4] A number of scholars have suggested that the lyrics that seem to speak of yearning for a heavenly home are actually a veiled reference to escape from slavery and a yearning for freedom in this life. Compare, for example, the lyrics to "Swing Low, Sweet Chariot," "Steal Away to Jesus," and "Soon I Will Be Done":

> Swing low, sweet chariot,
> Coming for to carry me home,
> Swing low, sweet chariot,
> Coming for to carry me home.[5]
>
> Steal away, steal away, steal away to Jesus,
> Steal away, steal away home,
> I ain't got long to stay here.[6]
>
> Soon I will be done with the troubles of the world,
> Troubles of the world, the troubles of the world,
> Soon I will be done with the troubles of the world.
> Goin' home to live with God.[7]

Each of these songs speaks of leaving one world for another world. Whether that world is an afterlife in a "spirit world" or a new life in a "northern world" of freedom, the archetypal energy invoked is that of the orisha Esu/Elegba, the deity of the road, the one who is said to "open the way" between worlds. As Jung explains it, every mythic figure corresponds to an inner psychic experience.[8] In this case, the mythic figure Esu/Elegba corresponds to the capacity to break boundaries and move between worlds, to live in the psychic space where worlds converge. The spirituals and the blues are cultural products of a people living at the crossroads, a people fighting to keep their souls from being "torn asunder." In the New World Lucumi system, the odu ruled by Esu/Elegba is Owani: "Owani is an odu very rooted in the past, yet fulfilled only in the present. . . . It incarnates great prophets, those who have the courage to deviate from the past in search of a better future."[9] The search for a better future, a brighter future, is prevalent in the lyrics cited above.

James Cone's popular work *The Spirituals and the Blues* substantiates this perspective. Through his focus on theological content, he points to the dehumanizing social conditions endured by Africans in America during the late eighteenth and nineteenth centuries and posits that those conditions created the experiences out of which the spirituals and the blues were born. Echoing W. E. B. Du Bois, he highlights the "tension in the spirituals," noting the seemingly contradictory themes of "hope and despair, joy and sorrow, death and life," and expresses fascination with "the ability of black slaves to embrace such polarities in their music."[10] Further exploring the concept of duality, Cone notes deceptive speech as a survival tactic and act of resistance: "To survive in an oppressive society, it is necessary to outsmart the oppressors and make them think you are what you *know* you are not. It is to make them believe that you accept their definitions of black and white. As one song puts it: 'got one mind for the boss to see; got another mind for what I know is me.' To be able to deceive the master was often the only means of freedom."[11]

Referring to the often-quoted phrase "No, massa, me no want to be free," Cone points to "the polarity of being and not being" that mere survival required of the enslaved African. He builds on John Lovell Jr.'s thorough account of how the "Afro-American spiritual was hammered out." Lovell defines the spiritual as a "folk song," a product of the "folk community," full of insider speech, "oral shorthand, symbol, meaningful but peculiar accent, irony, and significant silences," created to highlight matters of significance to the community from which it springs.[12] These matters of significance had to do with protection, secrecy, survival, and affirmation of self in a hostile world.[13] Throughout his discussion of the Afro-American spiritual as folk song, Lovell focuses on the "folk community that produced the spiritual," insisting that it was "African at its base and maintained its African attitudes and psychology in many ways."[14] Lovell describes the songs of a folk community as always the original expression of the community, bathed in its tradition and reflecting its image: "And because of the need for protecting the community's and each individual's precious thoughts and feelings, they are usually shaped through mask and irony."[15] This principle of mask and irony is what the Yoruba deity Esu/Elegba represents.

Samuel A. Floyd Jr., writing about the power of black music, draws from the "ring shout" theory of historian Sterling Stuckey and the "signifying monkey" theory of literary critic Henry Louis Gates Jr. For Floyd, the ring shout represents a fusion of sacred and secular, creating a space within which African Americans recognized and expressed their common musical memory through movement, sound, and gesture. His application of Gates's theory, using the signifying monkey motif, suggests a critical theory of black music that provides for analysis of the ways in which music reflects the "signifiers," the experiences of the people at the deepest level of emotion. In his words, music as signifying symbol indicates "that the musical tendencies, the mythological beliefs and assumptions, and the interpretive strategies of African Americans are the same as those that underlie the music of the homeland and that these tendencies and beliefs continue to exist as African cultural memory."[16] These underlying mythological beliefs and interpretive strategies are given voice through cultural memory expressed through various media.

And what of the blues? Cone refers to the blues as "secular spirituals," suggesting that it is the "affirmation of self" that connects them to the spirituals. In his words, "the blues tell us how black people affirmed their existence and refused to be destroyed by the oppressive environment: how, despite white definitions to the contrary, they defined their own somebodiness and realized that America was not their true home." He illustrates this point by quoting these lyrics:

> Ain't it hard to stumble,
> When you got no place to fall?
> In this whole wide world,
> I ain't got no place at all.[17]

These words reflect the experience of a people living in what Homi Bhabha calls an "unhomely world," full of ambiguities and ambivalences, fissures and splits.[18] Cone emphasizes the importance of looking beyond the hopelessness and despair to see that the blues also suggest that things will ultimately get better. He notes that buses, railroads, and trains, important images in the blues, symbolically represent the possibility of "leaving the harsh realities of an oppressive life."[19]

If we examine the Orisha tradition for comparable symbols, we find that the orisha Ogun is the deity associated with iron, metal, and mechanical operations: "Lord of the cutting edge, he is present in the speeding bullet or railway locomotive."[20] The symbols representing Ogun, including iron railroad spikes, a knife, and a metal toy car, are among the implements in the iron cauldron that initiates commonly receive.[21] The orisha Esu, also known as Elegba or Ellegua, is considered to be, among other things, the deity of the road, the one who opens the way. A closer look at these two orisha in relationship to the blues follows.

Ogun, Esu, and the Blues

Ogun is characterized as the warrior god, the one who forges implements that shape human destiny, the energy of motion and movement:

> The main tools of Ogun are the anvil, which signifies the earth's ability to transform [humans]; the hammer, which is used to bend or shape [one's] faculties; the machete, which is used to clear paths and to protect; the rake, . . . to smooth rough edges of the self; the hoe, . . . to cut weeds that would choke the cultivation of one's potential; . . . the pick . . . to pierce the hardened edges of the self; and the pry, . . . to uproot and remove stubborn obstacles from our paths . . . the history of the world is filled with examples of how most of these tools were used by various people in acts of war, defense, and basic survival.[22]

Anthropologist Sandra T. Barnes suggests that the above tools represent human triumph over limitations. She views the deity Ogun as a root metaphor for the quintessential marginal being as well as the one at the center of revolutionary and creative acts that give birth to new social forms.[23] It could be argued that the blues singer expresses such Ogun themes when capturing the energy and emotions of a people fighting for survival, struggling to move obstacles from the path of success, agency, and self-actualization. In his discussion of the blues as a secular spiritual, James Cone suggests that "the blues were techniques of survival and expressions of courage. . . . about the contradictions that black people experienced and what they did to overcome them."[24] The following are among the lyrics cited by Cone to illustrate this point:

> I'm awful lonesome, all alone and blue,
> I'm awful lonesome, all alone and blue,
> Ain't got nobody to tell my troubles to.

This expression of despair and loneliness is not unlike the Ogun of the marginal being. A more hopeful tone is reflected in the following:

> Well, I'm going to buy me a little railroad of my own,
> Well, I'm going to buy me a little railroad *all* my *own*,
> Ain't going to let nobody ride but the chocolate-to-the-bone.

These lyrics recall the Ogun that is at the center of social transformation. The buses, the trains, the railroads represent Ogun energy stirring and moving to create a different and better world. Ogun owns the odu Ogunda. Ogunda is a hot, volatile, fierce sign with a transformative nature.[25]

Samuel Floyd refers to the blues as a "communications system," one that, like the spirituals, spoke in codes understood by those in "the ring" but indecipherable to those on the outside. According to Floyd, "the code itself is interpretive, traditionally taught to blues people by Esu, the African god of interpretation and connector of the people to their African past." He points out the difference between the mood expressed in the spirituals, which he refers to as a "communal testimony oriented toward the next world," and that expressed in the blues, "a personal statement about an individual's view of his or her current circumstances," suggesting that African Americans were no longer bemoaning their plight in the disguised lament of the spirituals, but recognizing a certain amount of autonomy and "release from the oppression of slavery."[26]

Floyd points again to the mythic figure at the crossroads, Esu, god of interpretation, as the patron deity of the blues musician, interpreting the mind and mood of the people caught in the in-betweenness of their dual cultural heritage. Floyd suggests that following emancipation, African Americans gradually shifted from a cosmos controlled by "black mythology" to one dominated by "individual determinism," resulting in an experience of psychological alienation. He writes, "This psychological alienation from cultural roots, on the one hand, and the rejection by white society, on the other, resulted for many black Southerners in a dismal gloom that was both evoked and lifted partially by turn-of-the-century bluesmen."[27] The blues singers, men and women, spoke of the everyday hard times of a post-slavery people seeking to reinvent themselves during the late nineteenth and early twentieth centuries.

Floyd also suggests that the blues musicians, endowed with the interpretive gifts of Esu, created their new musical expression as a remix, reinterpretation, and revision of the "calls, cries, and hollers of the field slaves and street vendors and from the spirituals of brush harbors and church houses."[28] Thus the bluesmen and -women were "cultural signifiers," reflecting the pain of people re-creating themselves. Consider the lyrics from "St. Louis Blues":

> I hate to see de evenin' sun go down
> I hate to see de evenin' sun go down

Cause mah baby, he done lef' dis town
Feelin' tomorrow lak I feel today
Feelin' tomorrow lak I feel today
I'll pack mah trunk, an' make mah getaway.[29]

Here the theme has shifted from the plaintive "longing for Heaven," as expressed in the spirituals, to personal emotional pain. However, the theme of traveling, of moving on and leaving a bad situation behind, is still prevalent. In Yoruba cosmology, this theme reflects the archetypal energy of several orisha, including Esu/Elegba, representing the road; Ogun, representing motion; and Oshun, representing hope.

The Oshun Archetype

Ibu aro—Oshun as the dawn of a new day, the light on the horizon, the orisha of hope—is an energy familiar to African American people. In several apatakis, or mythical tales, Oshun is the orisha who saves humanity. She carries the offering that convinces Olodumare to release the waters during a severe drought. She is the one who must be consulted and included when the sixteen male orisha fail in their attempts to develop and organize life on earth. She is responsible for making cowrie-shell divination available to the other orisha, and thus to humankind.[30] She is hope when all hope is lost.[31] This theme of hope is expressed in "Trouble in Mind":

Trouble in mind, I'm blue,
But I won't be blue always,
For the sun will shine in my back door someday.
Trouble in mind, that's true,
I have almost lost my mind;
Life ain't worth livin', feel like I could die,
I'm gonna lay my head on some lonesome railroad line,
Let the two nineteen train ease my troubled mind.
. . . .
I'm gonna lay my head
On that lonesome railroad track,
But when I hear the whistle,
Lord, I'm gonna pull it back. . . .
Well, trouble, oh trouble,

Trouble on my worried mind,
When you see me laughin',
I'm laughin' just to keep from cryin'.[32]

The "Trouble in Mind" blues reflects both despair and hope. The theme of hope expressed in the lyrics "Trouble in mind, I'm blue, but I won't be blue always," is consistent with the description of the archetypal Oshun energy often described by scholars and practitioners:

> Ọ̀ṣun is the òrìṣà who heals with cool water. When she is invoked her presence is felt to bring lightness and effervescence to illness, want, and gloom. Ọ̀ṣun's ability to heal is based on her sovereignty and her compassion. She is a warrior who can fight for her children and vanquish enemies visible and invisible.[33]

> Ochun counsels the devotee to incorporate conflicts and divisions to the point of dissolution in the flow of life. Ochun promises then, not peace and serenity, but generativity and dissolution, and within generativity and dissolution, an incandescently intensified experience of life and the world.[34]

She is healer, artist, mother, bringer of joy and laughter, consummate diplomat and reconciler, resource of grace, and connoisseur of that which has beauty and value. She is also the feminine principle of sensuality, of luxuriant sexual arousal, and the gratifying spirit that accompanies good food, good friends, and good times.[35]

Oshun is also considered the deity of love, and there are many blues songs about love, the loss of love, the longing for love, and so on. The odu Oche is associated with Oshun, the deity of love, money, eroticism, and fertility. Oche is feminine energy, sweet, bittersweet, powerful, and awe-inspiring.[36] The bittersweetness, despair, and hope represented by the deity Oshun are not unlike the emotions expressed in the legacy of the blues. In *Blues Legacies and Black Feminism*, Angela Davis observes that "the blues as a genre marked a point in African-American historical development when black communities seemed open to all sorts of new possibilities. It was a musical form whose implied celebration of exploration and transformation held a special meaning for African-American women. It offered them the possibility of challenging the social norms governing women's place within the community and within the society at large."[37] The blueswomen, by taking on the role of traveling performers singing about the raw emotions of life, moved beyond the domestic roles assigned to women and communicated hope for a new and different life. The blues singers thus expressed a sentiment consistent with the energy represented by Oshun.

Ogun, Oya, and Black Power

The orisha Ogun, described earlier as a warrior god, the one who forges implements to shape human destiny, represents an archetypal energy of cyclical or evolutionary change. Oya, the orisha of the wind, represents radical change: "She is the breeze that cools us, the draft that chills us, and the fury of the tempest. . . . Ọya is represented by revolution, and can be viewed as the power of progression or the power of reversal."[38] The first generation of orisha worshippers, those who embraced the traditions during the 1960s and 1970s, did so during a time of radical social change, a time when the winds of Oya were stirring and Ogun was shaping iron in new ways. This was the era of the Black Consciousness movement, the Black Arts movement, the Black Power movement, and the Black Panther Party, all characterized by a call for revolution.[39]

In nearly every case, the first generation of orisha worshippers among the participants in this study, those who embraced the practices in the '60s and '70s, identified themselves as cultural nationalists. Many of them were attracted to some aspect of "performing blackness" before they knew what orisha worship was all about, as the following interview excerpts suggest.

> I was walking down the street in Harlem and I heard someone playing African drums. I knew it wasn't coming from a church. I literally followed the sound of the drum and ended up at the Yoruba Temple. I was a dancer then and the drum called to me. I later found out what it was all about. I was initiated when I was 18 years old; that was in 1968.[40]

> I was in college in the '60s and was part of the African American Student Association. There was a group among us who always wore African clothing on Sunday and that caught my attention. I later met an older man in that group and found out he was a Yoruba priest. I started looking for more information and I found an article in the

> *Pittsburgh Courier* that listed a Yoruba Temple in New York and one in Gary, Indiana. During the next break I went home to Gary, Indiana, and I looked up the cultural center and met a man who had been dealing with African culture for a long time and was associated with Oba Ofuntala (who was at that time with the Yoruba Temple in New York). His name was Medehouchi Shongodeni and later I went to the Yoruba Temple in New York with him. . . .
>
> I think it was in 1969 when I got my first reading. I had an invitation to speak to the Black Student Union at Indiana University. It was pretty powerful. Louis Farrakhan had been there the day before. Oba Ofuntala came from New York and spoke. Afterwards he did readings for a group of students who were trying to get involved and wanted to incorporate African concepts into black nationalism. That's when I got my first reading. He told me that Obatala was my guardian orisha. He also said that he had been seeing a lot of Ogun/Oya people, people who would take up arms and destroy anything . . . I was actually initiated in 1978.[41]

These interviews give an indication of the cultural milieu during the time when African Americans began to embrace orisha worship. During the height of the Black Consciousness movement, nationalist ideology was a part of the public discourse. Examples can be found in the oratory and the literature of the time. For example, Malcolm X gave his famous speech "The Ballot or the Bullet" in April 1964, preceding the passage of the Voting Rights Act of 1965. He identified himself as a "black nationalist freedom fighter" and emphasized black nationalism as the political, economic, and social philosophy of self-help that would free twenty-two million "black victims of Americanism."[42] He was critical of the leadership of the civil rights movement and called for an infusion of black nationalist ideology and an expansion of the struggle from civil rights to human rights.[43] Malcolm saw a global community and espoused black nationalism as a moral philosophy. He became an icon for the Black Power movement before he was killed in 1965. Oba Oseijeman reports that not long before Malcolm's death, two of his bodyguards came to the Yoruba Temple for a "reading" on Malcolm. According to Oseijeman, when he divined, the odu that led was Osa Meiji, a volatile sign owned by Oya. Oseijeman says he told them, "Death is all around Malcolm. This is very serious. There are certain *ebos* that must be done."[44] This is an example of how the Odu, the sacred scripture, is not only at the center of orisha worship and cosmology but is also an integral part of the lives of practitioners. This scene also demonstrates the concept of orisha archetype as cultural form.

During this time of heightened black consciousness, many individuals assumed African names. The black poet Don L. Lee became Haki R. Madhubuti, LeRoi Jones became Amiri Baraka, and Walter Eugene King, the founder of Oyotunji Village, became Oba Ofuntala Oseijeman Adelabu Adefunmi I. Oseijeman, a self-proclaimed "renaissance man," established several organizations in New York in the 1950s and early '60s, including the Order of Damballah Hwedo Ancestor Priests in Harlem in 1955; the Shango Temple in 1959 (which was replaced by the Yoruba Temple and the African Theological Archministry in 1960); the Yoruba Academy for the Academic Study of Yoruba History, Religion, and Language in 1961; and the Ujamaa African Market in 1962.[45] Determined to recast the religion as an ancient African tradition and remove the veil of Catholicism, Oseijeman and a small group of followers moved from New York to South Carolina in 1970 and established Oyotunji African Village. The patron orisha of Oyotunji Village, Obatala, rules the odu Eji Ogbe, which is considered an odu of creation, of "the primal impulse for expansion, evolution, and ascension."[46] The fact that the founders of Oyotunji dedicated the community to the orisha Obatala indicates that they understood themselves to be pioneers and institution builders, nation builders inspired by a cultural tradition of empowerment. This look at Oyotunji Village in the context of the development of the Yoruba movement in America provides a concrete example of what it means to reinvent the self through the construction of a cultural memory and the appropriation of "scriptures" and related ritual practices.

3

DIVINING THE SELF

For the Yoruba religious practitioner, "it is the reading of the self (not the text[s]!) that is important and awe-ful—both illuminating and freeing and disrupting and frightening," as Vincent Wimbush describes it.[1] In this chapter I examine the concept of self in Yoruba thought and, through selected case studies, demonstrate the importance of the Odu, not as a text, but as a tool for self-assessment and agency. Nearly all of the twenty-one participants in this study named their early experiences with diviners who gave incredibly accurate readings as one of the factors that attracted them to the religion. When asked to elaborate, participants generally did not refer to the odu of a particular reading but to the diviner's narrative interpretation and prescription, as suggested in this interview:

Interviewer: What initially attracted you?

Respondent: I wasn't attracted to it [the religion] initially. I was going through some personal challenges in a relationship and I had some friends who were into natural medicines, herbs, etc. and they kept telling me I should get a reading. . . . I thought it was something like a psychic hotline so I wasn't interested. But my situation kept getting worse and I finally decided to go see this Babalosha that they kept telling me about. After getting a reading and seeing how some of the things the diviner said were really manifesting in my life, I really became more and more interested.

Interviewer: What stands out in your memory from that first reading?

Respondent: What stands out in my mind is the initial prayer in the Yoruba language, the beauty of it . . . and how it was something sacred and serious going on at that time . . . and just the whole process of someone telling you about your life and about future events and then to see them manifest. . . . I knew there was truth in it. It was something that resonated in my soul.

Interviewer: How did that impact you?

Respondent: It impacted me in such a way that I started calling Babalosha every day asking him about this culture and about this religion and the gods and the purpose of worshipping the ancestors. It became more intriguing as the days passed and as the things that came up in the divination began to manifest even more.[2]

Though the respondent does not mention the odu of this reading, clearly, he considered the reading very relevant.

The diviners themselves described cases where their readings spoke to people's lives in ways that they never imagined. Again, they emphasized the divination story and the assessment of the individual's life circumstances, rather than the odu. Such responses support the validity of the claim that the reading of the self, not the text, is most significant.

When I completed the initiation and the training and was ready to start divining I was young and I felt a great responsibility, like a doctor telling people about their life. I remember a woman came to me about her daughter's health. The daughter was sick. They almost carried her in. She sat in a chair drooped and listless. Her eyes were glazed over. I did the reading and then I began to do this ritual I had learned. I could see an immediate change in her. She sat up with new life and energy. I was standing behind her and I could actually feel this change. Later I received a letter from the lady thanking me. So, I said, "OK. Now I know I can do this."

Interviewer: What do you attribute the change to?

Respondent: The incantations, drawing down the spiritual energy . . . just like back in the day when the preachers would cry out, "Oh God, oh Jesus!" and they would get the people all roused up. They were calling forth the spiritual energy. It's the same thing.

Interviewer: Is it accurate to describe divination as a healing system?

Respondent: Yes, I would say that it is a form of healing. It's like going to a doctor and the doctor telling you what you should do.[3]

In each of the above cases, the client consulted a diviner for a "reading of self," i.e., what's going on in my life . . . and what can I do about my relationship problems? What's going on with my daughter? Is it a physical, emotional, or spiritual problem? These questions are not uncommon for Yoruba diviners, and through their initiations and training, they are prepared to deal with a complex philosophical and metaphysical understanding of the self.

And what, exactly, is the self in the Yoruba system of thought? As Awo Fá'lokun Fatunmbi explains it in *Ìbà'se Òrìsà*, "Tikara-eni is the Yoruba word for self . . . The concept refers to all those elements that make up the total person," including *ara* (the physical self), *egbe* (the emotional self), *ori* (the conscious self), *ori-inu* (the inner self), and *iponri* (the higher self.)[4] Fatunmbi asserts that the goal throughout life is to achieve and maintain alignment between the different elements of self in order to live a balanced, successful life and to access one's spiritual power, known as *ashe*, which is often translated as "the power to make things happen."

In Yoruba cosmology, everything has its own unique *ashe* or form of consciousness. In Yoruba mythology, according to Fatunmbi in *Ìbà'se Òrìsà*, the orisha Obatala—known as the King of the White Cloth, a symbol representing the power of light to manifest as matter—is considered one of the creative forces that shapes the individual *ori*, translated as "head" or "seat of consciousness" (41). Other forces assisting Obatala include Ajalamopin—the power of light to create us, said to be responsible for shaping the psychological aspects of the person—and Ogun, the Spirit of Iron, responsible for shaping the physical body (42). Other orisha are involved in the creative process, too, all representing a unique aspect of the self and "preserving both internal and external forms of potential that appear to be carried through generations of descendants" (43). Each orisha or spiritual force is said to "own" or "rule" an odu, suggesting that the odu is both sacred scripture and an integral and embodied part of the self.

Fatunmbi lists the second component of the self as the emotional self, referred to as *egbe*, often translated to mean "heart." The term also is used to refer to a ritual family, i.e., members of a group initiated by the same person. The use of the term *egbe* to refer to both the emotional self as well as a social grouping suggests that the unique form of energy that supports the "heart" of an individual also supports the "heart" of a group. The physical organ, "heart," is the *okan*, but in the center of it is the *egbe*, that part that regulates the flow of emotion (43–44).

The third component of the self is the *ori*, or the conscious self. As noted above, the word *ori* is often translated as "head," but Fatunmbi suggests that a more accurate understanding is "seat of consciousness." The *ori* is further divided into three components, the first of which is the *iwaju-ori*, the area of the forehead, considered to be the seat of divine inspiration in relationship to character. The second component of *ori* is *atari*, the top of the head, a source of spiritual power. This area of the head links the inner spirit with the transcendent dimension called *lai-lai*. One's consciousness, linked with *lai-lai*, produces an emotional experience of the mystical that defies explanation. The third source of spiritual power is the *ipako*, "located at the base of the skull, where the skull joins the neck. It is at this place that individual Forces of Nature (Orisha) merge with individual consciousness. The iwaju-ori allows for mystic vision and the ipako allows for possession" (45). The diviner at work is communicating with spirit through the *iwaju-ori*. The adherent in trance possession is communicating through the *ipako-ori*. In both cases, the orisha energy that exists within the self resonates with a corresponding orisha energy as it exists in the world.

The fourth component of self is called the *ori-inu*, the inner self. Fatunmbi describes it as "like a mystery within a mystery," or the elusive "self that dances in front of the self." He also identifies two elements of the *ori-inu*: *apara-inu*, translated as "the mark of inner being," defined as one's internal disposition toward the process of building good character, and *ori appere*, translated as "the pattern of consciousness" or "the sign of consciousness." In Yoruba cosmology, every individual chooses an energy pattern, an orisha, prior to birth that guides one's consciousness through life (thus the term "guardian orisha"). The guardian orisha owns a certain odu, which is also a unique energy pattern that may express itself in a variety of forms and is deeply embedded in the pattern of consciousness at the seat of the inner self (49–50).

The fifth component, the *iponri* or higher self, is considered a perfect double of the self that exists in *orun*, or the invisible realm. This esoteric concept suggests that all forms of consciousness evolve from a primal source. The ultimate goal is to bring the individual human consciousness into alignment with the transcendent higher consciousness from which all life evolves. The underlying metaphysical principle is that "*Iponri* (the higher self) is rooted to *Odu*, and the *Odu* is rooted to the Source of Creation which makes all things an extension of the One" (50). This intricate explanation of the self provides a basic frame of reference for understanding the philosophical basis undergirding the divination ritual and related "scripturalizing" practices of the Orisha tradition.[5]

In the Orisha tradition, the client consults a diviner for a reading for greater self-knowledge and self-understanding, whether in a crisis situation or not. The diviner, trained to access the Odu by casting cowrie shells, palm nuts, or the divining chain, is concerned with providing the client with an accurate interpretation of his or her life story at a particular moment in time. The diviner is, in effect, scanning the energy system of the client, noting outstanding features, imbalances, and potentialities. Following this diagnostic process, the diviner then provides a "prescription" for maintenance or "treatment," all designed to help the client live a balanced, harmonious life and make sense of it all.

Religious Phenomena and World-Making Dynamics

In his discussion of the interpretive history of African American engagements with the Bible, Vincent Wimbush posits a tripartite schema as a heuristic device for charting and understanding a complex set of sociocultural dynamics in the engagement of "sacred texts" in the construction and reconstruction of self and world. The three phases of his paradigm are (1) flight or deformation, described as a period of de-construction or movement away from; (2) formation or reconstruction, described as building from a site of cultural marronage, and (3) reform(ul)ation or reformation, described as "talkin' mumbo jumbo" or "following the neo-hoodoo way."[6] I contend that this paradigm provides a tool for understanding the world-making dynamics of the Orisha tradition, both on a personal or individual level and on a collective or communal level. This paradigm has a striking similarity to the hero/heroine's journey, "the quintessential story of mythology throughout the ages: the quest of a hero or heroine who willingly or unwillingly ventures beyond the known boundaries of the day, meets and defeats spectacular forces, then returns with some hard-won, precious gift."[7]

"The hero's public journey, through myth," as Clyde Ford explains, "has long been a marvelous metaphor for the soul's private journey through life."[8] Identifying three movements—departure, fulfillment, and return—generally found in all African hero/heroine adventures, Ford suggests that such myths provide the social stories that heal and the templates for grounding life in relationship: "When trauma confronts us, individually or collectively, myths are a way of re-establishing harmony in the wake of chaos."[9] I would suggest that the African American appropriation of the Orisha tradition provides rich and fertile ground for examining the process of "re-establishing harmony." Here we see a people who have drawn from an ancient mythology and a constructed cultural memory to devise a self and a worldview in accord with the "eternal mysteries of being."

According to an initiated priest with thirty-five years in the Orisha tradition, any client or practitioner "comes to the fullness of the religion with a story to tell. . . . It is the role of the priest to understand this story and help the client re-write it."[10] Commonly referred to as a "reading," divination is the means through which the client's story is revealed or interpreted. A client generally goes for "a reading" in search of help in coping with some troubling aspect of life. The priest/diviner consults the oracle by casting the divining chain (*opele*), throwing cowrie shells (*dilogun* or *obi*), reading cards, or using some other tool to determine what energies, what personal texts, are operative in the individual's life. This first phase is akin to what Wimbush refers to as "flight or deformation," and what Ford refers to as "departure."

Stage	Wimbush	Ford
1	Flight	Departure
2	Formation	Fulfillment
3	Reform(ul)ation	Return

The client, with the help of the priest/diviner, thus begins the mythical hero's journey. As the following personal story indicates, this is a journey of reconstructing the self. A close look at this story will reveal a number of signifying practices. I refer to the informant as "Beverly."

Case Study: Beverly's Story

> My introduction to the Yoruba religion, or the "Orisha tradition," as you call it, started with a friend who was researching the tradition. My friend began telling me about her fascination with the material she was reading and what she had learned from the priests she had talked with. At first, I was simply an interested conversational partner,

asking clarifying questions and more or less serving as a sounding board. I had grown up as a Christian and I had answered the call to "ordained ministry." So, of course, I was a bit leery and skeptical about what I was getting into. But I was drawn to it because I was feeling like I needed some other spiritual avenues through which to express myself.

I had always had what I call a keenly sensitive spiritual self. I dreamed a lot and had visions sometimes even when I was not asleep. I didn't know what to do with this, and I thought perhaps I could find some answers and some help by exploring this tradition. So when my friend called and told me that one of the Yoruba priests would be at her house on Saturday evening, without hesitation, I told her I would be there. This was my first reading. It was just a little over a year ago. My life has changed; I mean my life has really changed since then. The first thing the priest said to me was, "You know spirits." I was a little puzzled and I didn't say anything. He said, "There are lots of spirits around you. You have lots of dreams. You can't be getting anything out of all that." Then he cast the divining chain and he said, "Oh, we can't go any further. We have to stop here because it says you are at war with the mothers. You will need a head feeding."

I had no idea what he was talking about. I think I might have said something like, "So what should I do?" He said, "Well, I will try to find someone locally to work with you, a priestess." He gave me his phone number and told me to call him in a couple of weeks. After several weeks we finally connected, and he gave me the name and phone number of a local priest to contact. This priest was supposed to find a priestess to "work with me," but after he wasn't able to identify anyone he agreed to work with me himself. After several phone conversations, I scheduled an appointment for a reading.

Then I began to get nervous, but with my friend's prodding decided to go anyway. When I walked in, I felt this powerful energy in the room. It was an energy that I had not felt before. It was amazing. We sat on the mat and he threw the shells, made some marks on a paper, and began to tell me things about myself. I didn't get the answers that I was seeking, but he gave so much other information that I felt like help was on the way. He told me to go to the doctor, actually, to go to a gynecologist because there was a problem that needed attention. I already had an appointment with the gynecologist. I wasn't concerned or alarmed, but I was excited that he was able to tell me this. I was impressed. I was curious. A whole new world had opened up to me in that moment.

During the reading he started talking about some spirits or energies that were speaking to him. So I wanted to know about those spirits or energies. I didn't ask him any questions at that time because I was so excited. Afterwards, I did go to the doctor, and I learned that I had several fibroid tumors that needed to be removed. I decided to have the surgery, but before scheduling it I went back to the priest for another reading because I wanted to ask him to get more information from the oracle or those spirits or whoever was doing the talking. But I didn't even have a chance to ask my question, for as soon as I sat on the mat and he threw the shells, he said, "So when are you going to have your surgery?" That's the first thing he said. . . .

My curiosity was piqued and I wanted to learn more about the spirits and the ancestors. One of the prescriptions was to set up an altar to the ancestors and to two or three of the orisha that he said were guiding me. After I set up the altars I felt connected or re-connected in some way, or like the repair of a breach or something that was lost and was beginning to be found. I really felt like I was recapturing something that was lost ages ago. It seems like a whirlwind of changes happened after those first readings. I had no fear or anxiety about the surgery. I had a sense of peace before and after the surgery, such that people were saying there was something different about me, a kind of light and brightness.

I felt an internal shift, but I wasn't quite sure what the changes were. I felt strong and a new sense of possibility. I felt like my life was going to take a new turn. I guess I felt like this was the closest I had come to knowing my life's purpose and destiny. So this gave me a new sense of resolve, to live life fully. But the journey has been difficult. I've participated in two other rituals. I received the *elekes* and the warriors. But the past few months have been difficult. I've experienced a lot of spiritual unrest. I felt like I was wrestling, struggling to break through some resistance, but I knew it was not going to last forever.

Now, it feels like this difficult period is past and I'm ready for the next thing, the initiation into the religion. I'm excited about it and I think it will help usher me into getting those answers I was seeking. My life is changed. I'm more connected to myself because I'm connected to the ancestors. I think this is providing an avenue for me to

> use my spiritual expression in new ways. My whole sense of self as a black person living in this country has been fragmented. So having the ancestral connection is really a big thing. It's like glue that allows me to put myself together and to be whole.[11]

This is one person's story about the construction of self. A closer look at Beverly's story reveals both elements of Wimbush's tripartite schema for African American engagement of "sacred texts" as well as Ford's mythological paradigm. Phase one, deconstruction or departure, starts with Beverly's self-assessment: "I was drawn to it [the Yoruba religion] because I was feeling like I needed some other spiritual avenues through which to express myself." Beverly's remark represents what Wimbush would call "flight" or "deconstruction," and what Ford would refer to as "departure." When the opportunity presented itself, Beverly consulted a priest/diviner for a "reading of self." She said that the diviner cast the chain (the *opele*) and made some marks on a paper. Those "marks" represented an odu. The reading is, in effect, an interpretation of the energy active in a person's life. The diviner's initial assessment was a one-line interpretation of Beverly's life story: "You know spirits." He expounded upon that theme: "There are lots of spirits around you. You have lots of dreams. You can't be getting anything out of all that." Then came the second part of the reading: the prescription, a course of action for rewriting the story, reconstructing the self. He advised further consultation and work with a priestess. In this story, the "signifying practices," both explicit and implied, include divination, altar construction, and participation in ritual and ceremony. All are aspects of reconstructing self and world.

Divination and Rewriting the Story/Reconstructing the Self

John Mbiti, in *African Religions and Philosophy*, writes that in "the art of divination . . . a certain amount of communication goes on between diviners and non-human powers (whether living or otherwise or both). It is difficult to know exactly what this communication is—it might involve the diviner's extra-sensory ability, it may involve spiritual agents, it might be telepathy, it might be sharpened human perception, or a combination of these possibilities."[12] The Yoruba divination system, as explained by practitioners, opens the way for the gods to speak and creates the possibility for the co-creation of something new in one's life.

As one priest commented, "With every cast of the *dilogun*, a new text is written, for the priest offers an interpretation unique to the client."[13] In one of Beverly's divination sessions, the priest told her the following story: "Obatala and Legba prayed to the gods for money, and their prayers were answered. But Obatala put his money in his pockets, which had holes in them. As he went about his business, he lost all of his money through the holes in his pocket. Legba kept his money in a safe place. Hold on to any money that you get. Be careful how you spend." This divination narrative uses the metaphor of pockets with holes to suggest that the client should be careful about her spending practices. While the narrative offers Beverly specific guidance and advice about her life, the interpretation and practical application is up to her.

Divination is a part of each phase in the paradigms outlined above, as a client continues to work with the priest. Beverly's follow-up work begins phase two, referred to as "formation" in Wimbush's schema or "fulfillment" in Ford's. This is a time of building and establishing self in a new and different space. According to Ford's mythological template, Beverly is the heroine who has been called forth from the familiar to the unknown into an "ontological journey" of self. She will meet various challenges in this new territory, this liminal space. Beverly alludes to such challenges in some of her comments.

> The journey has been difficult. . . . I've experienced a lot of spiritual unrest. I felt like I was wrestling, struggling to break through some resistance, but I knew it was not going to last forever.
>
> Now, it feels like this difficult period is past . . . My life is changed. I'm more connected to myself because I'm connected to the ancestors. . . . My whole sense of self as a black person living in this country has been fragmented. So having the ancestral connection is really a big thing. It's like glue that allows me to put myself together and to be whole.

Beverly speaks of change and a sense of "connectedness" heretofore missing in her life. The story suggests that she has experienced a time of despair followed by a breakthrough and is about to enter another phase, one of reintegration, reformulation, return. She comments that she is looking forward to the next step—initiation into the religion—because she believes that she will find more answers to her quest for understanding herself and her life's purpose.

What elements were involved in this reconstruction of self? Though she did not elaborate these activities in her account, Beverly mentions setting up altars and participating in ceremonies, rituals that, in the Orisha tradition, are essential to the reconstruction of self. A more detailed discussion follows.

Ceremony and Ritual

According to Lionel Scott and Hermes Torres, "the Orisha tradition is a psycho-social-spiritual healing, evolutionary system [that] can bring about changes in body, mind, and spirit on an individual as well as a communal level."[14] As they explain it, ceremony is one of the ways through which an individual can open the portal to the realm of spirit and connect with "orisha energy" to bring about change or restore alignment. Other methods include storytelling, ritual, dancing, and drumming—all activities, or signifying practices, that help people understand and develop rapport with orisha energy.

Through Beverly's story, we hear her narrative voice, a particular projection of self. The narrative account is one that spans a period of time, giving a broad representation of what transpired. But different genres speak in different voices and give different projections of the self.[15] What voice is projected through ceremony in the Orisha tradition? Scott and Torres suggest that in Orisha ceremonies, certain distinguishing drum rhythms and *oriki* chants are used to attract particular energies, create certain moods, and evoke specific responses. John Mason, a priest of Obatala and an accomplished musician, confirms the "indispensable role" of music in the Yoruba religion. Amazed by the fact that Cubans, African Americans, and Puerto Ricans were so moved by the sonic/spirit power of song and dance that they memorized hundreds of songs in a language they did not know or understand, Mason collected, translated, and published *Orin Òrìṣà: Songs for Selected Heads*. The volume includes songs and chants for each of the major orisha. Of the task of the master drummer and lead singer, Mason writes,

> both the master drummer and master/lead singer study and employ the use of *tratado*, the Spanish word for *treatise/discourse*. The *tratado* is a "played/sung" narrative: account, story, tale that treats a subject, discussing and exposing it in a systematic manner and proceeding

> in an orderly and logical sequence. In Yorùbá, discourse would be described as ọ̀rọ̀ sísọ tọn (speaking statements that are related), or Ìwásù (preaching, sermon), or Ìwáàdí (examination, investigation). The tratado system is a mnemonic device . . . intended to assist the memory of important historic persons, places, events and times.[16]

Mason further notes that through the medium of sound, the drummer/singer is able to evoke and direct tremendously potent psychic forces. This could explain why many of the participants in this study said that they were first involved in the music and dance before they began to embrace the religion. Of the twenty-one persons who participated in the study, eight of them mentioned music, drumming, and dance as major factors that drew them to the religion. One person commented that while she was growing up in the Catholic Church, she learned that "one song is worth seven prayers," and she firmly believes in the power of song. She sings nearly every weekend for a *bembe*—a party or celebration—in New York.[17]

In his discussion of "entangled voices," Frederick Ruf suggests that the lyric voice reflects the self at the deepest, most intimate level.[18] For example, a moan tells us something that a story does not. When a prayer is chanted or an *oriki* sung, another aspect of self is projected. Only the "thick description" of an astute ethnographer might adequately describe such a voice.[19] Language need not be a barrier to understanding the projection of the self through the voice, as I realized in my own experience as a participant observer in Orisha ceremonies. For example, one Sunday morning in Sheldon, South Carolina, my friend "Beverly," my brother, and I were at a Best Western hotel waiting for one of the senior priests of Oyotunji Village to return for a scheduled meeting with us. Tiring of waiting, we decided to drive over to the Village—only about a mile down the road—and walk around the grounds. We drove down a bumpy, winding dirt road through the trees, parked the car, and entered just as the tour guide was telling two visitors that if they hurried, they would be able to watch part of a ceremony. He motioned for us to come quickly and follow him. He led us toward an enclosed ritual space with an open entrance area where we could stand and peer in. Several men and women were singing and chanting to the music of the drums and other traditional instruments. They were dressed in traditional African attire in white and wore red stoles draped across their shoulders. They were speaking in Yoruba, and for the most part, I did not understand what they were saying. I was, however, able to decipher one phrase, and it was uttered with such reverence and emotion that I knew a prayer had been spoken. The words were "adupe, baba, adupe." I whispered to Beverly, "I think she is praying. She just said, 'thank you, father, thank you.'" Even though I did not understand the language, I understood the presence created by the words spoken. In witnessing this ceremony, I had recognized the power of the lyric voice. However, the power was not in the words alone, but in the context, in the embodiment, and in the performance.[20]

Attending these ceremonies is generally a part of the re-creation and establishment of the self in the religious tradition. According to Scott and Torres, ceremony is one of the ways through which practitioners develop a rapport with orisha energy. Experienced musicians know how to pace the music, and they know which beats and which tones are used to evoke each orisha. When an orisha possesses a devotee and speaks to the guests, the speaking voice is not always the same, but movement and gesture are universal. The participants recognize the orisha energy communicating through these characteristic movements. The embodied voice thus makes a difference. Scott and Torres remind us that even though "it may appear that one is building a rapport with something outside yourself, you are really building an inner rapport. It is by tapping the Orisha energy within that one can better understand the information."[21]

This rapport with orisha energy starts with a ceremony that marks one's formal entrance into the religion. In the Lucumi tradition, this initial ceremony, one that Beverly alluded to in her story, is referred to as "receiving the *elekes*" or "the beads." Beverly received five strands of beads, each a different color configuration, representing each of five major deities. But just as important as the beads themselves is the ritual process by which they are received. The terminology "receive" is significant and seems to place the recipient in a passive role, which is only partially true. The initiate is also an active participant, and the ritual process represents a kind of self-transformation.

The first phase of this process is a form of "departure" from the old self. The initiate is "washed" with a special herbal mixture, and the old clothes are torn or cut off and discarded. The initiate is dressed in white and, after participating in a ritual behind closed doors, shares a meal with her new ritual family. But she is considered a "baby" now and must sit on the floor and eat her food with a spoon. The plate, the floor, the spoon, and the white dress are ordinary objects, but here in ritual context they acquire special meanings. As studies of cultural performance have pointed out, "Meaning is not latent in ritual signs and awaiting discovery; instead, people involved in ritual performances engage signs and activate them."[22]

This ritual marks the beginning of a new understanding of self, and it establishes a new set of social relationships. The priest from whom Beverly received her *elekes* becomes her "godfather," a kind of teacher, mentor, and role model. The priest is responsible, to a great extent, for Beverly's growth and development in the religion, for much of the learning is not "cognitive" but experiential, relational, and communal. Beverly's godfather trains her the way his godmother trained him, a brief description of which follows: "564 Amsterdam Avenue, New York City, New York . . . Mercedes Nobles, Obanjoko, sits in her apartment delegating, instructing, and commanding, attracting, creating and recreating her 'Pueblo,' an enriching community . . . a culture in raw creation. . . . each individual representing a thread in the fabric of her ever-evolving community."[23]

Beverly will have subsequent divination readings from her godfather and will consult with him for guidance in interpreting and understanding dreams and other vectors of spiritual knowledge. The "godfather" and "godmother" will play significant roles in helping Beverly develop proficiency in "reading" self and "re-storying" life. Beverly contacts her godfather on a weekly basis to find out whether he has information or prescriptions for her. Generally, he tells her the result of her "energy reading" for the week but does not discuss the odus that came forth in divination, which again supports the point that significance lies less in the "text" than in the person.

4

SYMBOLS AND SIGNPOSTS FOR THE JOURNEY

What do ritual symbols mean? How is such meaning communicated? How do the symbols accomplish social and psychological transformations? In addressing these questions, Edward L. Schieffelin disagrees with the premise that symbols are effective because they somehow make sense of particular problematic cultural or psychological situations and then lead the participant to a new framing of the situation, a premise widely held by the Saussurean school of thought. He argues instead that "symbols are effective less because they communicate meaning . . . than because . . . meanings are formulated in a social rather than cognitive space."[1] As opposed to the Saussurean school, which argues that meaning is derived from language and abstract webs of significance, Schieffelin looks back to Charles Sanders Peirce's more contextual practice-based perspective on symbol, suggesting that humans engage in semiosis as they continuously represent and interpret reality. My analysis of Beverly's story fits well within this framework. Peirce suggested that signs do not exist in isolation but are always connected to other signs and have the capacity to generate new signs.[2]

In the case study described above, Beverly mentions setting up altars and establishing connections with her ancestors as very significant aspects of her life. This act itself is symbolic and is filled with other sign/symbol objects that point to yet other signs and symbols that reflect her worldview and perspective on life. What problematic cultural or psychological situation has been addressed? For Beverly, it was a feeling of alienation, fragmentation, and disconnection. Establishing an altar for one's ancestors is considered very important in the Orisha tradition. Such rituals of remembrance are integral to Yoruba cosmology and indicate the cultural value placed on the "birth, death, rebirth" life cycle. Death is considered a moment of transition from one form to another, material to spirit, from embodied to disembodied existence. Orisha traditions teach that ancestral spirits can be accessed and engaged as support in the vicissitudes of life. Beverly established a basic ancestral altar, which included one or more glasses of water, a white candle, pictures of her deceased mother and father, a Bible, and, sometimes, freshly cut flowers, all attractively arranged on a shelf covered with a white cloth. She prays in front of the altar and seeks guidance from the spirits of her ancestors. One of her deceased relatives often appears in her dreams. Her "godfather" has told her not to be afraid of shadows or of feeling a "presence" in her room, for accepting and understanding this phenomenon is a part of her spiritual development. Thus the ancestral altar is a critical part of Beverly's reconstruction of self.

In addition to ancestral altars, Orisha practitioners also establish altars for their most important deities, particularly their guardian orisha, the one who is said to rule the "head," the center of spiritual life. In one of her readings, Beverly's "godfather" told her that she was a child of Oshun and should find ways to engage the energy of Oshun. After several informal conversations, Beverly learned that "Oshun is creativity, sensuality, sexuality, joy, and love. Her number is five; her symbols include the peacock, the catfish, the pineapple, as well as combs, mirrors, and brass bangles; her colors are yellow and orange."[3] Using items from this list, Beverly erected an altar to Oshun and included more "Oshun colors" in her wardrobe as well as her home décor. In these ways she began to "embody" the Orisha traditions, reflecting not only a new understanding of self but also a new expression of the energy matrix called "Oshun." Not only has Beverly changed, then, but so has the Oshun text. While Beverly focused on a fixed interpretation, in actuality, the Oshun principle expressed in culture is expansive, adaptive, and varied. What we see here is an integration of myth and ritual, signs and symbols in aspects of personal development as well as in the transmission of culture and the expansion of social knowledge.

In explaining this phenomenon, Clyde Ford suggests that the orisha should be viewed "as personifications of those archetypal energies that manifest in nature and within human life." Ford goes on to state that "the individual, through ritual address, possesses the gods and goddesses as a way of repossessing those essential, divine aspects of one's self."[4] Wole

Soyinka refers to these archetypal energies of the Yoruba deities as "essence-ideals," reflecting the self.[5] Drawing examples from the Yoruba pantheon to illustrate his point, Soyinka focuses on Ogun, who, in Yoruba mythology, is considered the one who cuts through obstacles along the road of life.

In the ontological journey of self, Ogun is the one who clears the road of inner and outer obstacles standing in the way of personal and social change. As Soyinka tells the story, there was once only one "godhead" in Yoruba mythology. This primogenitor god was attended by a servant, Atunde, who became angry one day and decided to seek revenge by smashing God into many pieces by rolling a boulder down the mountain. Thus the one God became many gods, known today as orisha. In time, the orisha began to long for oneness and realized that the experience of oneness could be achieved only by uniting with humans, with whom they shared a common ancestry. In order to accomplish this goal, Soyinka explains,

> [there had to be a] journey across the void to drink at the fount of mortality though, some myths suggest, it was really to inspect humanity and see if the world peopled by the mortal shards from the common ancestor was indeed thriving. But the void had become impenetrable. A long isolation from the world of men had created an impassable barrier which they tried, but failed, to demolish. Ogun finally took over. Armed with the first technical instrument which he had forged from the ore of mountain-wombs, he cleared the primordial jungle, plunged through the abyss and called on the others to follow. . . .
>
> . . . Ogun is the embodiment of challenge, the Promethean instinct in man, constantly at the service of society for its full self-realisation. Hence his role of explorer through primordial chaos, which he conquered, then bridged, with the aid of the artifacts of his science. The other deities following through the realm of transition could only share vicariously in the original experience. Only Ogun experienced the process of being literally torn asunder in cosmic winds, of rescuing himself from the precarious edge of total dissolution by harnessing the untouched part of himself, the will. . . . [Thus] it is as a paradigm of this experience of dissolution and re-integration that the actor in the ritual of archetypes can be understood.[6]

The journey and its direction are at the heart of the divine/human relationship in Yoruba cosmology. The deities/orisha represent archetypal energies engaged in the ontological journey of self. The *guerreros* ritual, or the "receiving of the warriors," one of the ceremonies Beverly referred to in her story, is an important part of the Orisha tradition. In her case, the "warriors" included symbolic objects representing Esu/Elegba (a small cement head-shaped figure), Ochoosi (the archer's bow and arrow), and Ogun (metal tools—knife, rake, shovel, and the like). Every morning she prays that Elegba will open her roads, that Ochoosi will point her in the right direction, and that Ogun will clear away any obstacles. As Beverly engages the sacred in this way, she could be viewed as an actor in the play of "ritual archetypes," involved in a journey of self, experiencing challenges and hardships and receiving new information for reflection and integration.[7]

As Margaret Thompson Drewal points out in *Yoruba Ritual*, the journey metaphor is used extensively in the organization of Yoruba thought, and the Orisha tradition employs it in a variety of ways. Noticing how often she recognized the journey motif in the stories narrated by ancient diviners, Drewal posed the following question: "Are all rituals journeys?" (31). Her diviner friend answers her by telling another story and then by pointing out that she (Drewal) herself is one of the actors on the journey, so, he wonders, how can she ask if they are all journeys? Drewal posits that wherever Yoruba religion thrives, throughout the Diaspora, the journey motif is expressed in myriad ways—in narratives, in ritual performances, in possession trance—and always illuminates the experiences of day-to-day living (33). The journey always represents some kind of change or progression.

As an example, Drewal points to her work with Ositola, a Nigerian diviner and ritual specialist who shared with her the following explanation of an important sacred ritual:

> All people who go to the sacred bush (*igbodu*) benefit from it. They may be observers; they may be priests; they may be initiates. Only we concentrate on the initiate most. Yet everybody is involved, particularly the priests, for there is a belief—and it's an agreement between ourselves and Odu (the deity) within the sacred bush—that we are reborning ourselves. Even we priests, we are getting another rebirth. At every ritual, we are becoming new because we have something to reflect upon. We have something to contemplate during the journey, at the journey, after the journey. Our brains become sharper. We become new to the world. We *do* there, and we *see* there. And even more simply we pray for everybody. (37–38)

This is but one example of ritual performance embodying the characteristics of a journey—particularly its tripartite movement of separation, liminality, and re-aggregation (ibid.).[8] In the Yoruba traditions we also find the journey motif in the ceremony referred to as "stepping into the world," performed following the birth of a child, and in "knowing the head," performed within the infant's first three months. These ceremonies serve to identify the child's *ori*, or personality, and learn the nature of the *emi*, or spirit/soul.[9] In each of these rituals, the diviner "reads" and reveals the Odu that pertains to the child, and, in consultation with the parents, offers an interpretation. This interpretation becomes a significant part of establishing the child's identity and constructing the sense of self, for it serves as a guiding principle in the adults' caretaking decisions. In other words, such readings provide guideposts for the journey.

The same journey motif can be applied to the history of a people. Imagining the African American experience as that of a single character, Clyde Ford writes, "thinking of my character's survival of the Middle Passage, 'a dark sea journey' comes to mind; and of his suffering during slavery, 'the dark night of the soul'; and did he not enter 'the belly of the beast' to battle for freedom, justice, and equality in America? These phrases bespeak the journey of a hero."[10] Ford continues to support his argument by relaying a story told by the BaKongo people about their ancestors who were captured and sold to white men who enslaved them. The captured people were said to have been taken to the island of Mputu, a place where, in the mythological literature of the region, hero figures travel, struggle with dark powers and magical beings, and fight for treasures to bring home to their community. Eventually the gods and goddesses intervene and provide assistance. So in the minds of the BaKongo people, Ford explains, African Americans are hero-souls of ancestors, and they will return home again, as all heroes must.[11] The following summary of a story told by an African American Orisha priest speaks to the questions at hand:

> Once there was an old wine merchant named Obamoro who lived alone with his dog, Besi, and his cat, Obi, in a small village along the bank of a river. The three were great friends and understood each other completely. Obamoro sold wine to all the travelers and ferrymen who passed his door, and he was known for having the sweetest wine in all the land. He lived comfortably until a long drought brought hard times. After a while, neither villagers nor travelers had

money with which to buy wine, but Obamoro graciously extended credit to all who came to his door. Besi and Obi did not approve of this way of doing business, especially when they noticed that their food portions were getting smaller and smaller.

Finally the day came when there was not a morsel of food left to eat. The old man sat huddled in his hut with his two companions, wondering what would become of him. Suddenly there was a knock at the door. With a glimmer of hope in his eyes, Obamoro rose stiffly and made his way to the door. A finely dressed stranger had come for wine. Obamoro greeted him warmly, invited him in, and brought out his last jar of wine. He poured from it, hoping that there would be enough to fill the bowl. But when he poured the last drop, the bowl was only half full. The stranger jumped to his feet and started for the door. Obamoro jumped in front of him, apologized profusely, and explained that he had given his all. After a long silence the stranger stretched out his hand, revealing an amber stone. He dropped the stone into the wine jar and commanded the old man to pour. Obamoro was astonished to find the wine jar full to the brim.

The old wine merchant's jar never became empty, no matter how much he poured from it, until one day he poured and there was no more. He immediately realized what had happened. He had accidentally poured the amber stone into someone else's jar. Hard times were approaching once again. He inquired around the village, but no one acknowledged having seen the amber talisman. Besi and Obi took it upon themselves to join in the search and eventually spotted the glimmer of the stone shining through a crack in the thatched roof of a village hut on the other side of the river. With the help of their animal friends they were able to retrieve it, but they lost it again while crossing the river to get back home. By this time Besi and Obi were no longer friends and they parted ways. But Besi was determined not to abandon the old man. So every day and every night she lay on the bank of the river, keeping careful watch on the very spot where she had dropped the precious stone. One day she saw a fisherman pull a huge catch from the water. As soon as he landed it, Besi grabbed the largest fish and quickly ran to the old man's hut.[12]

Lionel Scott and Hermes Torres's narration of "The Magic Amber" concludes this way: "Anyone can guess the rest of the story. How the magic amber dropped out of the fish when the old man cut it open; how he ran to his empty wine jars and put the talisman in with trembling fingers; how the sparkling wine bubbled to the top of the jar; and how Obamoro made a fortune once again."

Knowing the social context of this sacred text is crucial to an analysis of its function.[13] In the sense used here, the social context is a process of self-shaping through practices that are fluid, flexible, and emergent (though practitioners may often make statements that suggest a fixed perspective in reference to the archetypal characteristics of the orisha). The story is a summary of an apataki, or sacred story, published by two New York City Yoruba priests. It comes from the odu Eyeunele Obara, a sacred text of the Lucumi tradition, and has been transmitted orally from one generation to the next. Eyeunele is represented by a configuration of eight open mouths and eight closed mouths on the mat, i.e., eight shells facing up and eight shells facing down when the cowrie shells are thrown by the diviner. It is said to be the oldest odu of the *dilogun*. Obara is represented by six open mouths on the mat. (This configuration is sometimes called Eji Ogbe.)[14]

The story of the amber talisman is only one of many associated with this odu and is a kind of "signification" on the text, for the narrative chosen for symbolic representation of the text is always left to the interpretive choice of the diviner. The priest/narrator informed me that he divined to find out which story he should write about for a recent publication. The configuration that fell is a sign for the odu Eyeunele Obara, and the amber talisman is the story, from the storehouse of his memory, that he associates with this sign. Such a story, he says, would serve as a reference point, a guidepost throughout life for a person whose ita reading included this sign. From time to time, contemplating various scenarios in his or her life, the person would ask particular questions, e.g., "Who am I now? What character am I in the story? Am I the dog? Am I the cat? Am I the winemaker?"[15]

The story of the amber talisman was not randomly chosen, I am told, but reflects the current status of the Yoruba/Lucumi religion. The priests/leaders are concerned about the future of the religion. Some within their ranks tenaciously hold on to the traditional ways of doing things, while others believe that change is necessary for the religion to attract new adherents in the twenty-first century.[16] For them, this mythic text functions to highlight the relationship of tradition and innovation. Besi, the dog, represents tradition; Obi, the cat, represents innovation. At one time the two could coexist peaceably, but Obi's self-centeredness caused an irreparable breach. Scott and Torres suggest that this apataki reflects contemporary times in the religion.[17]

The mythic "hero/heroine's journey" motif is also present in this story. The dog, Besi, is the hero who leaves home in search of the treasure—the amber talisman—and encounters difficulties, challenges, and hardships, yet finally returns with it. The tripartite structure is clear, and it could speak to either individual or collective self-understanding. Scott and Torres use the story to reflect the concerns of a social group, i.e., the community of Yoruba/Lucumi religious practitioners. But the psychological aspects of the story could just as easily have implications for individual self-understanding in terms of the challenges of reconstructing the self, of rewriting the personal story. The river is the chasm that must be crossed, the challenges that must be faced, in order for the individual to reach a point of fulfillment and individuation.

What might this story say about how the African American "hero/heroine souls" are faring in the mythological land of Mputu? Have they survived the challenges and hardships of the land? Have they found the amber talisman? Have they returned home with a treasure? Have the gods intervened to provide assistance? Applying the Wimbush/Ford three-phase paradigm of the hero's journey, we examine these questions through the lens of the Orisha tradition as embodied by the Yoruba practitioners of Oyotunji Village.

Case Study: Oyotunji Village

The historical record has it that the village was started by an African American practitioner who was initiated into the Orisha tradition in Cuba in 1959. Disgruntled and disillusioned with the tradition called Santo practiced by Cuban Americans in New York City, Oseijeman Adefunmi (Walter Eugene King) vowed to create an independent African society where the traditional Yoruba culture could be practiced without the veil of the Catholic saints, thereby proudly reclaiming the sacred wisdom of ancient Africa.[18] This stance led to controversy within the membership of the New York City Yoruba Temple in the latter part of the 1960s and to Oseijeman's eventual separation from the group in 1969.

This separation and departure marked a new phase of Oseijeman's journey as well as a new phase of the African American development of what might be termed a new religious movement. The road to Oyotunji Village was fraught with hardship and difficulty. Indeed, the Village was started only after another pursuit failed. Oseijeman had been offered a position teaching African history at a North Carolina school called Transitional

Academy, established by a church group to help students with academic deficiencies prepare for college.[19] He left New York, accompanied by one of his four wives, Majile Olafemi, and her two children, and moved to North Carolina, only to realize that the school was poorly funded and doomed to failure. Through divination he learned that "Oya, the Goddess of Death, had doomed the program."[20]

However, he interpreted this experience as the work of the orisha to get him to move to the South. After wandering about for a bit, he and his family settled in Savannah, Georgia, and were joined by several other members of the New York Yoruba community. After experiencing many financial difficulties and personal conflicts, the group decided to leave Savannah. The question "Why can't the orishas do something?," posed by Majile Olafemi, served as a catalyst for this move. It forced Oseijeman to determine how orisha energies might be engaged in day-to-day experiences, and shortly afterward the group was able to acquire land in Paiges Point, South Carolina. They settled there and built small huts along with temples, shrines, altars, and houses for ancestor worship.[21]

In the words of one of the members of the founding group, "We built the shrines and temples as a living monument to our African ancestors. We realized it was time for us to do something or this part of our history would be forgotten."[22] These shrines and temples, then, were a way of constructing a usable cultural memory. One of the ways that societies remember is through ritual performance and bodily memory, both aspects of initiation in the Orisha tradition.[23] As the group became settled, people began to come for initiations, and although Oseijeman was inexperienced, he agreed that it was time to take on this responsibility. Carl Hunt, the first historian to write the story of Oyotunji Village, describes the initiation ritual as follows: "The first part of the initiation took place at night at the river near Paiges Point. As they left the house to make their way to the river, a terrible storm broke out and everyone was frightened but Baba. . . . Baba was able to spur them on by recounting the events of the night of the Haitian revolution which began during a great storm. . . . He told them, 'The sky was celebrating that revolution and now it is celebrating ours. We must go on.'"[24]

At the river they plunged the initiates in the water, ripped off their old clothes, bathed them with an herbal mixture, and dressed them in white. Afterward, they returned to the village. According to reports, "the storm ended and the night became beautiful and clear."[25] The initiates stayed isolated in a room for seven days, after which time they emerged and rejoined society as new beings with new names. The initiation ritual speaks to a reconstruction, a reinvention of self. The initiates were submerged in water to wash away the old and dressed in white to symbolize a new and pure beginning.

The trip to the river could be interpreted as phase one of the journey, a separation or departure. The seven-day period of isolation in the temple room is the second phase, a time of liminality. Upon the completion of all of the initiation rituals and ceremonies, the person returns to society for reintegration as a new person with a new social status. This ritual would be repeated many times at Oyotunji Village. For an individual experiencing it, it was a milestone on the road of the ontological journey of self, but this first Yoruba initiation in South Carolina had another meaning as well: "the Yoruba had started a new departure for Black Americans. They had finally reclaimed their religion. . . . They were actually reproducing it on American soil. They had decided to manage and reorganize it to suit their own needs and lifestyles."[26]

Many of the new initiates left to resume their lives in other cities, and others were socialized into life at Oyotunji Village. Persons who wanted to establish residency in the Village were expected to follow certain residency requirements, adhere to spiritual guidance based on a priest/diviner's divination to determine the ruling orisha, take a vow of allegiance, and agree to the rules that governed the community. The following three rules were considered very important: (1) all villagers must wear African attire at all times, (2) all men must work on the *dokpwe* (public work groups), and (3) all persons living in Oyotunji Village must receive tribal marks within three months.[27] These rules, particularly the first and third, indicate the strong emphasis placed on the establishment of a group identity.

Oyotunji Village, then, could be seen as the third phase of the African American hero/heroine's journey, which, according to both the Ford and the Wimbush paradigms, is a period of remixing traditions. In spite of the struggles, the failures, and the battles that were won and lost, it seems that the hero/heroines of African ancestry have fared well in the mythic land of Mputu. They have "recovered the amber talisman" by reclaiming and reconstructing a cultural memory, and by doing so they have exercised a sense of social power and agency.

The Oyotunji story is a fascinating one, but it is not as strange as it might seem. Since their forced arrival, many Africans in America have turned to the sacred to redefine the self and remake the world. The history of oppression and its resistance is replete with examples of African Americans gathering sacred cultural resources to create meaning in a hostile environment and to refashion their lives. Mechal Sobel's study of the religious history of enslaved and freed Africans in antebellum America reveals, for example, the centrality of the spiritual experience in the shaping of an African American people. Sobel maps the journey from an enslaved African sacred cosmos to what she calls an "Afro-Baptist faith."[28] Likewise, Albert J. Raboteau, in his discussion of the history of slave religion, examines the "death of the African gods" but also points to the survival of African spiritual practices in song, dance, story, and ritual.[29] Following the same line of thought, Vincent L. Wimbush focuses on the history of African American engagements with the Bible and how this language world enabled African Americans to negotiate everyday life.[30] The founders of Oyotunji Village, by comparison, moved from the Christian "scriptures" to the Yoruba "scriptures," employing African cultural resources to help contend with life and reinvent the self.

Emerging Issues

A number of important issues related to the "performative" aspects of religion surface in the above discussion. These issues include (1) the role of performance in the imaginative construction of cultural memory, (2) the politics of culture in terms of what elements of a culture are acknowledged and recognized, (3) the epistemological function of divination narratives, (4) the exercise of agency through the performance of ritual and ceremony, and (5) how personal and cultural identity might be transformed through performance.[31]

In their discussion of performance, culture, and identity, Elizabeth Fine and Jean Haskell Speer argue that "when the cultural or physical landscape is torn, or when circumstances wrench people from their homelands, performance provides a way to recover that physical space through the imaginative reconstruction of a cultural landscape."[32] Though it could be argued that present-day African Americans were never wrenched from their home lands, the social history of slavery and oppression has led many to construct an imagined homeland. The above case studies suggest that the Orisha tradition provides some African Americans with an arena for the construction of an imagined homeland based on the Yoruba cultural landscape and worldview. For example, Beverly commented that as an African American, she had always felt that a part of herself was missing. She said she felt like someone who had been away from home for so long that she had forgotten the way back. But her involvement with Yoruba religious practices had provided a missing link for her, reconnecting her to an ancient, ancestral heritage. Other participants in the study expressed similar views:

> Deciding to go forward with initiation was a big issue of faith for me because I still didn't know much about these people in the religion and I had to trust that everything would be OK. When I heard the songs it all seemed so familiar to me, like something I had always known, but I hadn't. I felt like I was reborn and renewed. I had tried different churches and different denominations. . . . Baptist, Methodist, Pentecostal, Catholic, but now I finally felt like I was home.[33]

> For me this is a way of life. It was not a choice. I know that home is home and there's nothing better than home. This religion is home for me. I know nothing better. This was here before I started going to church. This was here while I was going to church and this was here when I stopped going to church. If I decide to go back this will still be here. This is where my heart is. This is home. And I hope and pray that the religion will become the beautiful thing it is meant to be.[34]

The Yoruba priest from Oyotunji Village commented that they built the shrines for the African gods lest the culture be forgotten. Oseijeman, the founder of Oyotunji Village, broke away from the Afro-Cuban practice known as Santo, Santeria, or Lucumi because he wanted to establish a practice that was, in his estimation, more authentically African. He was initiated into the Ifa priesthood in Nigeria in 1972.[35]

The documented history of African American religious practices focuses primarily on Christianity. For example, Milton C. Sernett's edited volume *Afro-American Religious History: A Documentary Witness* includes, out of fifty-one documents, only three on African religions. Only one of these three focuses on America, and it is on the subject of conjuration and witchcraft.[36] Likewise, Fulop and Raboteau's collection *African American Religion: Interpretive Essays in History and Culture* offers little in the way of information on African-derived religious practices. Out of a total of twenty essays, the collection includes only one on "conjure and magic" and one on Ogu in Haiti.[37] As Anthony Pinn has noted, there is a serious gap in the literature on African American religious expression and practice.[38]

Pinn suggests that the African American theological focus on Christianity establishes Christian doctrine and concerns as normative and thus limits understanding of the complexities of African American religious practice, expressions, and experience.[39] The fact that the Orisha tradition has often been practiced in concealment, too, results in fewer historical documents being available. But even the scarcity of sources is a reflection of the politics of culture at work.

Such politics dictate the norm, and those practices that fall outside of the norm are distrusted. One who engages in such practices or performances thus takes a countercultural stance. Divination, an epistemological tool that lies at the very heart of the Orisha tradition, is seen as a suspicious activity, even though it may provide an alternative way of knowing self, culture, and others more completely. Even a cursory look at divination suggests paying attention to the signs, symbols, and practices of religion as important "cultural texts." This act, in and of itself, falls outside the norm for scholars of religion who have been trained to privilege a canon of printed documents as the basis for interpreting religion.

But when a performance paradigm is employed, it shifts our gaze to the phenomenology of religion, including the experiencing body in cultural context. And in the examples cited above, we get a glimpse of the significance of embodied experience in re-creating self and world. Fine and Speer note that "studying performance . . . is a critical way for grasping how persons choose to present themselves, how they construct their identity, and ultimately, how they embody, reflect and construct their culture."[40] Certainly, it follows that studying persons engaging the sacred—performing, enacting, embodying that which is deemed sacred—speaks volumes about what one values and how one constructs self and culture. In the final analysis, it is the reading of self and selves that is "important and awe-ful—both illuminating and freeing and disrupting and frightening."[41]

5

POWERS OF THE MOTHERS

The babalawo cast his chain and looked up. "You have a pretty good destiny reading," he said. "The only thing that could keep it from happening is . . ." He hesitated, then dropped his voice to a whisper: "the mothers."[1] Seated on the mat across from him, I, at this precise moment, began the quest for a greater understanding of the Yoruba/Orisha concept of "the mothers" and its expression in contemporary African American culture. I found the mothers—veiled, covered, shrouded in secrecy, wielding an unspeakable power—a terrifying, shape-shifting, signifying, hoodooing, conjuring culture power. The mothers create, destroy, and form worlds anew. In this chapter I examine related mythology, rituals, symbols, and systems of thought.

According to some of the Ifa divination mythology, the very name of the Yoruba sacred "scriptures," Odu Ifa, comes from the "Great Mother," the divine feminine Oduduwa. Oduduwa is translated as "Oracular Utterance Created Existence."[2] Legend has it that Oduduwa was a wife of Orunmila, the god of destiny. She gave birth to sixteen children who became the sixteen primary Odu, the communication link to the realm of spirit. She then taught her husband the art of divination. Oduduwa, praised as Yewajobi, the mother of all orisha and all living things, is referred to as the womb of creation, the feminine energy principle from which all things emerge. She is the owner of *aje*, a power that, according to Teresa Washington, is a "signifying, hoodooing, conjuring" force evident in the worlds Africans throughout the Diaspora have created for themselves.[3] Though the term *aje* may be used to refer to a spirit being, a spiritual power, or a spiritually powerful woman, Washington focuses on aje as creative force. She finds evidence of this multifaceted, multidimensional spiritual power in literary and other cultural texts that express an uncanny drive to create life anew. Using Washington's definition as a frame of reference, this chapter discusses the concept of aje and its role in selected apatakis. It also examines rituals and symbols associated with three of the most popular female orisha: Oshun, Yemonja, and Oya. Relating such roles to the Ford/Wimbush social formation paradigm, I focus on how aje as creative force is expressed in the context of "signifying, hoodooing, and conjuring" African American culture.

Aje

Washington uses the term *aje* to refer to the "furtive force the Great Mother [Iyami] used to create life and ensure evolution. She shared her force . . . [to] ensure that the world maintains its structure and balance." The term is also frequently translated as "the witches," or "the mothers," and the mothers are referred to as witches. "The Mothers . . . shhhh." During the course of my fieldwork, practitioners literally spoke the term in a hushed whisper, if they mentioned it at all. When I could summon the courage to ask, my inquiry met with the response, "The mothers are so powerful that we don't speak of them. They must sanction everything or it won't happen." Once when I asked how I could find out more about "the mothers," a diviner said, "No one talks about them or writes about them. I know one priestess who worships 'the mothers.' She knows the energy and how to work it, but the last I heard, she had lost her mind."[4]

A young woman, on another occasion, reported that in a reading a babalawo told her that she was an aje, commonly called a witch, but that *aje* was not necessarily a negative term. He said it meant that she had a very powerful will and should be careful about her thoughts because she had the power to make things happen. When she inquired as to how she could learn more about the aje, she was instructed to wait until the right teacher could be found. After several follow-up phone calls, she decided that her efforts were futile and dropped the matter altogether.[5] This conversation stimulated my curiosity and inspired me to continue my search to discover more about "the mothers."

My perusal of the literature found Wande Abimbola suggesting that one of the most powerful images of women in Ifa literature is the depiction of women as aje, or witch, "a blood-sucking, wicked, dreadful cannibal who transforms herself into a bird at night and flies to distant places, to hold nocturnal meetings with her fellow witches."[6] Abimbola elaborates by explaining that in the Yoruba concept of a universe divided into two opposing camps, the left-hand side represents malevolent forces, while the right-hand side represents benevolent forces. Women are said to occupy positions in both camps, on the left as aje, and on the right as human beings. Thus women are viewed as liminal beings, "endowed with certain supernatural powers."[7] As Abimbola further explains, "All humans who aspire to positions of power, or who have already been vested with powers and authority must honor, salute, and pay homage to the *àjẹ́* who are fondly remembered as *ìyàmi*—'my mother.' All the positive and negative powers of the earth flow from the *ìyàmi*."[8]

Abimbola acknowledges that there are many other images of women in the Ifa literature—as mothers, as wives, women in the marketplace, and so on. He concludes that the literature reflects a love-hate relationship between Yoruba men and women but points to the fact that all important meetings and transactions include women's authentic involvement, because everyone knows that the inclusion of women is necessary for balance in the universe and access to supernatural power.

Aina Olomo, an African American practitioner, goes a step further by pointing out that every odu reflects the birth and the outcome of a particular set of circumstances, indicating a natural link between Iyami Odu as mother of creation and Orunmila as god of destiny. She cites the following *ese* Ifa that establishes the relationship between the two: "You trample on the bush. I trample on the bush. We trample on the bush together."[9] Taken from the orature of the odu Irete Ogbe, this verse, according to Olomo, suggests that the bush symbolizes the barriers and challenges of life, the obstructions that Orunmila and Iyami together are able to defeat, reflecting the power of manifestation and transformation. Olomo points to the confusion and fear that surround the concept of "the mothers" among African American practitioners, positing that it stems from a lack of understanding of what the power actually means and what it entails. She calls for the development of a philosophical and theological understanding of this feminine energy power base so that it might be used for a form of spiritual activism with the potential for social transformation.

Acknowledging the difficulty of conceptualizing this multidimensional African spiritual power, Washington uses such terms as "ubiquitous, ambiguous, and invisible," defining aje as everything and nothing simultaneously. Noting that the term refers to both a spiritual power and spiritually empowered humans, she suggests that this furtive, resilient power is elusive, defies logic, and challenges the religious imagination. Washington engages the symbolism of myth and metaphor to communicate the essence of what many practitioners have perceived as so powerful that they dare not call the name. She finds evidence of aje's influence on ritual, drama, orature, music, visual arts, and literature and points to Zora Neale Hurston's *Mules and Men* as a brilliant example of how this aje influence appears in African American culture. However, it could be argued that the *Mules and Men* text does not imply any Yoruba influences on African American literary expression, but rather shows how the use of such a text can function in the African American construction of a Yoruba ancestry. Perhaps Washington projects her own values onto the text and finds them there. Engaging a bit of aje herself, Washington describes the importance of Hurston's works to her own understanding of this creative power in action: "Hurston's works became artistic and critical roots that moved stones of Western ideology out of my path. She also lent me her shoes with the sky-blue bottoms so I could fly to Nigeria and better understand the power inherent in Africana women that makes it a forgone conclusion that they will create and recreate and texture, color, and enliven nearly everything they touch no matter where they are."[10] Washington finds in Hurston an expression of feminine power that parallels the Yoruba concept of aje.

To locate this aje power in the mythology and religious practice of African American orisha worshippers, I will examine anecdotal evidence from field observations and interviews along with selected apatakis, rituals, and symbols associated with three popular female orisha: Oshun, Yemonja, and Oya. Each is considered to have a "road," or aspect, that represents "the mothers." I argue that in the final analysis it has been the aje, the feminine energy principle as the power to re-create one's world, that African American orisha worshippers have found most alluring and compelling. Ironically, this is the factor least discussed among practitioners.

Working the Mother

Reflecting the numerology of Oya, Luisah Teish identifies "nine works" that women can engage in to reclaim knowledge and power and bring about personal and social change. These nine works include the following: (1) household magic, (2) personal power, (3) charms and chants, (4) loving the earth,

(5) reconnecting roots, (6) rituals for extended family, (7) the seven African powers, (8) Jambalaya, and (9) working the rainbow.[11] Each work includes recipes, rituals, chants, and/or stories that the practitioner is encouraged to use to effect desired changes in particular circumstances. Collectively, Teish refers to these activities as "working the mother."[12] Her prescriptions are based on the belief that all things in the universe are connected and have a spiritual significance. Thus, words are uttered or rituals performed to invoke, awaken, strengthen, balance, or replenish the *ashe*, i.e., life-force energy, that will affect the situation in question.

In this manner, Teish teaches women to recognize and utilize a form of feminine power based on energy and rooted in the human psyche. Her practical application of Orisha tradition is consistent with the black feminist thought of Patricia Hill Collins, whose scholarship focuses on "knowledge, consciousness, and the politics of empowerment."[13] In Collins's words, "Black feminist thought aims to develop a theory that is emancipatory and reflective and which can aid African American women's struggle against oppression."[14] In the strategies suggested by Teish, this struggle is on the level of individual consciousness. She urges women to accept the responsibility of transforming self and environment. "Come, Sisters," she says, "take this journey with me, share this responsibility with me. . . . are you willing to serve in the house of the Mother?"[15] To "serve in the house of the mother" means cultivating one's intuitive faculties, embracing one's power, or defining one's self.

Serving in the house of the mother is equivalent to what Collins refers to as rejecting theories of power based on domination and "embracing an alternative vision of power based on a humanist vision of self-actualization, self-definition, and self-determination."[16] Collins also argues that "offering subordinate groups new knowledge about their own experiences can be empowering. But revealing new ways of knowing that allow subordinate groups to define their own reality has far greater implications."[17]

This, in effect, is what the Orisha tradition is all about, embracing a new/old way of knowing. This alternative way draws its knowledge from "women's ways of knowing," from intuitive thought, from dreams, from nature—from the deep recesses of the human psyche. This alternative way of knowing is performative in nature, rich in symbol, ritual, and metaphor. As Teish explains it, "Symbols work because they evoke responses that lie deep within the human psyche. They affect the subconscious and turn the consciousness wheel to produce an appropriate response."[18] In this worldview, the life force "passes through us, is used by us, and must be replenished by ritualistic means. Replenishing the *ache* is a prime reason for the existence of individual and group rituals and the use of charms."[19] All things in the universe are connected—the plant, animal, and mineral kingdoms—and all have an effect on each other: "Words uttered in a particular sequence, rhythm, and tone can bring a rock to 'action,' cause rain to fall, or heal a sick person a hundred miles away."[20]

Of the perfomative nature of the practice and the power of the oral tradition, Aina Olomo writes, "the meanings of words exist in our hearts and are born from the passion of our spirit. When they pass from our lips they create energy that is transformed into the ability to do work."[21] Olomo expresses concern about trends that seem to suggest that New World practitioners are beginning to replace spiritual exploration with memorized quotation. "In my own journey," she says, "I learned from powerful elders who have shared their wisdom with me; they never read books on Ifa, nor did they quote oracle to their fellow seekers like western 'scriptures.'"[22] The concern that Olomo expresses has to do with what is and is not an acceptable form for the transmission of knowledge. Her comments suggest that there is something in "spiritual exploration" that cannot be found in the printed word. She says the meaning comes from the "spirit in the heart" producing a transformative energy through the spoken word.

The sentiments expressed by Olomo are consistent with those of bell hooks, the well-known black feminist scholar and cultural critic. Referring to her book *Sisters of the Yam*, hooks says it, like all of her writing, comes from places "dark and deep within, secret, mysterious places, where the ancestors dwell, along with countless spirits and angels."[23] She grew up learning that everything in life is a dwelling place for spirit; hooks also saw that black women worked with at least as much skill, power, and second sight as their black male counterparts. In *Sisters of the Yam*, hooks writes that when she left this environment for a predominantly white university, she took with her those "ways of knowing and understanding reality" (9). This statement implies that her ways of "knowing and understanding reality" were different from the ways of the university. Those ways that she took with her, that sustained her at the university and continue to fuel her work and her life, are aspects of the Orisha tradition and are performative in nature. She posits that the forces of domination have wounded the "hearts, minds, bodies, and spirits" of black people: "A culture of domination undermines individuals' capacity to assert meaningful agency in their lives. It is necessarily a culture of addiction, since it socializes as many people as it can to believe that they cannot rely on themselves to meet even their basic human needs" (68).

So hooks issues a call for black people—and black women in particular—to engage in self-recovery as a liberative political practice, suggesting that "choosing wellness is an act of political resistance." According to her prescription, knowing one's self and where one comes from is the first step to recovery, and it necessitates finding "a space within and without," where one can "sustain the will to be well and create affirmative habits of being" (14). In discussing her awareness of and sensitivity to the psychological health of African Americans, hooks refers to a passage in Toni Cade Bambara's novel *The Salt Eaters*, where the black women ancestors come together to talk about healing the character who has attempted suicide. One of them poses the question, "What is wrong, Old Wife? What is happening to the daughters of the yam? Seem like they just don't know how to draw up the powers from the deep like before."[24] Inspired by this passage, hooks organized a young women's support group which she named "Sisters of the Yam." She was shocked when black female students came into her office to reveal that they were plagued by problems of low self-esteem, domestic violence, and fear of failure. The Sisters of the Yam support group became a safe space where students could reveal their psychological pain and seek healing in community (12).[25]

"I also felt the 'yam' was a life-sustaining symbol of our diasporic connections," hooks writes. "Yams provide nourishment for the body as food yet they are also used medicinally—to heal the body" (13).[26] In further explaining how the group functioned, hooks comments that the power of the group to transform each other's lives seemed to hinge on each individual's desire for and commitment to wholeness. She gives great credence to the power of an affirmative response to the question posed by the black woman healer in *The Salt Eaters:* "Are you sure, sweetheart, that you want to be well?"[27] Only an affirmative response brings with it the power to transform and reinvent self.

As noted above, hooks suggests that one of the strategies for well-being is knowing how to "draw up the powers from the deep." Indeed, this is a central theme in the Yoruba Orisha tradition as practiced by African Americans. The diviner relies on the "powers of the deep" when interpreting the Odu and providing a narrative that applies to the client's life. When practitioners said that the tradition gave them a feeling of finally "coming home," they were connecting with an inner power source. The orisha

Oshun, Yemonja, and Oya, constructed as feminine energy, manifestations of aje, represent various aspects of those "deep powers within" that practitioners draw upon to reinvent self and world. A reflection on the Odu, the mythology, and the symbol system surrounding each indicates that these three female orisha cover the cycle of life from birth to death.

In fact, their mythological roles are so powerful that one might expect more visibility for women in the religion. Some have suggested that women in the Orisha tradition have been taught to fear their own power, while others suggest that those who embrace the psychology of female power may reclaim their power through an understanding of the metaphysical principles that undergird the practice. Still others have been completely turned off by the sexist and patriarchal attitudes they have seen expressed by practitioners.[28]

In spite of the diverse opinions regarding gender tension and the "power of the mothers" as expressed in the archetypal constructions of these three female orisha, we have seen that the feminine energy principle is an integral part of the Odu. Odu Ifa, the oracle itself, is said to be the Divine Mother's gift to the world. Known both as Oduduwa (Oracular Utterance Given Existence) and Iyami (My Mother), the concept of the archetypal mother is at the center of both Ifa and *mirindilogun* (sixteen-cowrie-shell) divination, for every situation the Odu addresses has a life cycle that includes a birth, a continuance, and an end. Oshun is associated with birth and is said to be the owner of cowrie-shell divination. Yemonja is associated with care and life-maintenance activities, and Oya is associated with death or radical change. Thus the feminine energy principle operates on both the physical and metaphysical levels and is central to the African American practice of the Yoruba Orisha tradition. As we have seen, author/practitioner Luisah Teish refers to this process as "working the mother." Teresa Washington describes it as an African American way of engaging "our mothers, our powers, our texts" in the active process of signifying, hoodooing, and conjuring culture to make life anew in the face of oppression. Such practice is performative in nature, embraces alternative ways of knowing, and engages feminine power at the level of the human psyche with the goal of self-actualization, self-definition, and self-determination in mind.[29]

6

OSHUN, YEMONJA, AND OYA

In the Yoruba pantheon, the deity Oshun is characterized as the personification of fertility. The word *oshun* means "source." In the words of Joseph Murphy and Mei-Mei Sanford, "Ọ̀ṣun is the perpetually renewing source of life, . . . the appearance of sweet water from dry ground, a mode of hope and agency in new and difficult situations, a way out of no way."[1] Her symbols are the beaded comb, the mirror, the peacock, and honey. Her number is five. Her colors are yellow and gold. She owns the odu Oche, under which it is said that all things small become great and powerful; under its effects, even the greatest mountain can be felled. Oshun is considered to be the river goddess, the owner of fresh water and the guardian of mystery.[2]

As the guardian of mystery, she is credited with having made the *mirindilogun* system of divination available to all the other orisha and to the people of the earth. Legend has it that whenever the people of the earth (*ikole aye*) wanted the guidance of divination, they had to go to Obatala, for he alone possessed the knowledge of *mirindilogun*. But often when the people came looking for him, he was nowhere to be found. Oshun, the river goddess, took it upon herself to do something to change the situation.

One day she decided to follow Obatala and see what she could do to make the system of divination available to the Omo Orisha (children of or followers of Orisha). When Obatala left home, she followed him to the river and watched as he took off his sparkling white robes and left them in the brush along the banks of the river so that he could bathe. Oshun saw Obatala's friend Esu (the divine messenger) standing nearby and asked him if he could convince Obatala to teach her the art of divination. Esu immediately replied that she should go home and bathe in *oyin* (honey). Esu then picked up Obatala's clothes and took them to Oshun's house. When Obatala finished his river bath, he came out of the water only to discover that his clothes were missing. He followed Esu's tracks, which led him from the river to Oshun's house. He knocked on Oshun's door, and she answered the door dripping in honey. She agreed to give Obatala his clothes back if he would teach her the art of *mirindilogun* divination. Thus, "by using her allure and charm, *Oshun* makes divination available to all the Immortals."[3] In another version of this story, Oshun is the wife of Orunmila, and he teaches her the art of divination so that she might help the people in his absence. How does this myth function in traditional and contemporary societies?

In his commentary on the symbolism in this story, Fatunmbi notes that the river is the source of fresh water. He further points out that water nourishes vegetation, nourishes the embryo in the womb, is necessary for life, and maintains ecological balance. In his words, "*Oshun* as the incarnation of both fertility and love represents the impulse to maintain balance and harmony within the natural environment. When this impulse is translated into a communal environment, it represents the motivating factor for social justice. . . . In traditional Yoruba political structure it is the priestess of *Oshun* who has a key role in maintaining the communal standards of justice and equality."[4]

In this story, Oshun not only uses her charms but also elicits help from Esu, the trickster, to acquire and redistribute the power wrought by the ability to divine. What is the significance of the art of divination? This study suggests that it provides the capacity to know one's self and one's world more completely. It is a tool for self-exploration and social analysis. For any given situation, it is not only diagnostic but prescriptive as well, suggesting that with the knowledge and skill of divination, people are able to exercise agency in their individual and communal lives. Here the female power principle, aje, is at the very center of the capacity to re-create one's world.

Another apataki that speaks to this theme is entitled "Hidden Power: Ọṣun, the 'Seventeenth *Odù*,'" or "Seventeenth Orisha." This story speaks of how, in the beginning of time, when the earth was just being formed, the creator god sent seventeen Odu from the invisible realm of heaven to make the earth inhabitable for humankind. Oshun was the only female among them. When the Odu arrived, they went about the business of establishing their separate domains and deciding how they would complete their mission on earth, but they did not include Oshun in any of their plans. For a while things went well, but before long, problems began to develop. Rain did not fall, crops did not grow, epidemics spread, the earth was barren, there was no healing in the land, and life became nearly unbearable. Oshun stood quietly by and watched. They did not know that she was aje.[5]

They went from place to place seeking solutions, but to no avail. They even went to Oshun, but were too proud to ask for her help. Finally they decided that their only alternative was to go back to Olodumare and admit failure. When they arrived, they told Olodumare that nothing was working on earth. Olodumare asked a few simple questions. "How many of you are here?" "Sixteen," they replied. "How many did I send to earth?" They answered, "Seventeen." "There's your answer," replied Olodumare. "Unless you include Oshun, nothing will be successful. Everything you attempt will fail." The sixteen returned to earth and sought out Oshun to tell her that they had been to visit Olodumare.[6]

They told her that they now realized what a horrible mistake they had made, and they begged her to come out and help them. They told her that they did not know that she was the mother of all Odu. Oshun said that she had been aware of their mistake all along, and she knew of all the good foods they had eaten without her and all the activity they had not shared with her. She was not forgiving. They kept pleading with her, though, and finally she told them that if her unborn child were a male, then she would help them. However, if her unborn child were a female, she would not help. The sixteen began to pray that Oshun would give birth to a male child, and she did. She named the baby Osetura, known also as Esu, and he became known as the divine messenger, the one who bears sacrifice to all of the orisha, and the embodiment of the element of uncertainty in Yoruba culture.[7] In another version of this story, the male orisha, Ogun (Spirit of Iron), Ochoosi (the Hunter), and Shango (Spirit of Lightning) bring all of their implements and lay them down before Oshun, acknowledging her indispensable power and authority. In this story we again see the significance of aje as the female power principle. The sixteen male orisha are powerless against the one female.

In *Mythography*, William Doty poses critical questions for the study of myth, including questions about the relationship of myths to "gendering" and to "aspects of the psyche/personality/self" as well as the community.[8] Such questions are particularly significant in analyzing this apataki.

Oshun's power was not visible to the male orisha; however, as the story unfolded, it became clear that their success depended upon her cooperation. Rowland Abiodun, commenting on the symbolism of the Oshun concept, points out that Oshun is the "hair plaiter" and the owner of the "beaded comb." Oshun adorns the outer head, but she also is said to be the one who controls the *ori*, i.e., the inner head as the seat of consciousness—and consequently one's destiny.[9] On the eve of every initiation, it is customary that the priests request Oshun's approval of the candidate before performing any part of the initiation ceremony. Even though the candidate's readiness for initiation is ascertained long before any preparations are made, in the Lucumi system, the godparent and *ajubona* (second godparent) will come together at an appointed time to pose the question in a formal way. While this may appear to be a formal, fixed, and repetitive action, in practice it is emergent and active. Catherine Bell's notion of ritualization offers an appropriate theoretical frame of reference for understanding this pattern.[10] The Yoruba priests themselves acknowledge variations in the acceptable protocol, though they often argue for an established and "acceptable" way of conducting a ceremony. One priest uses the following initiation questions:

> Godparent: Who approves this candidate for initiation?
> *Ajubona*: Upon investigation, the community and I approve.
> Godparent: Who has been consulted on the worthiness of the candidate?
> *Ajubona*: Oshun has been consulted and approves the worthiness of the candidate.
> Godparent: Then let us proceed.[11]

In the language of the priesthood, an initiation "makes the head" of the candidate. The fact that the goddess Oshun is consulted before every "head" is made indicates the importance of the feminine energy matrix. This again shows how "the mothers" regulate everything that comes into existence—even priests and priestesses. Oshun, the goddess of fertility, is the principle that gives life.

In considering what aspects of the self the "hidden power" mythic text addresses, I consulted several practitioners who reminded me to consider the Orisha iconographic symbols and what they represent. In one version of the story, Ogun relinquishes the tools used to cultivate the land (the hoe, the rake, the pick). Ochoosi turns over the bow and arrow that he uses for the hunt, and Shango relinquishes the double-edged ax. The act of turning these tools of "self-development" over to Oshun suggests that the mystical, hidden power of the self, deeply seated in one's consciousness, one's *ori*, ultimately governs one's life. The implements owned by the male orisha are important tools for clearing the inner landscape of barriers and obstacles or self-defeating tendencies so that creative, fertile, productive, and life-sustaining energies might flow.[12]

Gender complementarity is also a theme here. Oyeronke Oyewumi reminds us that the Yoruba language is not gender-specific. Since a people's language reflects their patterns of social behavior, the absence of gender specificity reflects the extent to which sex differences in Yorubaland do not form the basis of social categories.[13] In support of this point, she notes that the words "son," "daughter," "brother," and "sister" have no Yoruba equivalents, indicating that social roles are not based on such gendered kinship terms but rather on seniority.[14]

Likewise, seniority is a theme reflected in much of the mythology. The Odu are assigned a rank order based on seniority, that is, in terms of how in the mythic history they entered the world. This order has a particular meaning for the interpretation of divination. Seniority also plays a role in the ordering of the orisha. Oshun is considered the youngest orisha, yet one of the most prominent and most powerful. In African American practices, the priesthood protocol recognizes seniority as an organizing principle; the number of years one has been initiated serves as an important criterion of status and respect. One indicator of this organizing principle in operation is the fact that during communal meals, priests are served in rank order according to years of initiation, with the persons on the bottom rung acting as "servers." In addition to differences constructed along seniority in "New World" practices, we also find differences constructed according to gender, in spite of the gender complementarity found in the mythic history and traditional practices. Both in the Lucumi and the Ifa systems, the role of ritual leader is generally reserved for males. In the Lucumi system, the oriate leads all ceremonies associated with initiation. In the Lucumi communities I studied in New York, there were no female oriates; however, there were female equivalents to the babalawo in the Ifa system as practiced at Oyotunji Village. It is my understanding that some communities (both in West Africa and in America) initiate women as *iyalawo* and *iyanifa*, and some do not. The society of ritual drummers is also male. When asked about the practice of excluding women, participants in the study commented that it was a matter of the different *ashe*, or energy, that males and females bring to the ritual process; they did not speak of it as a sexist or discriminatory practice. It seems that most roles that explicitly use the aje of women have not survived in America.[15]

In her work on Yoruba women in the religious sphere, Oyeronke Olajubu argues that "gender classifications were present in precontact Yoruba society, but they were culture bound."[16] She turns to the function of the two gender-based cults for information on gender roles in Yoruba thought systems, reporting that the predominantly female cult, *iya mi*, was "concerned about the sustenance of the ritual powers on which the Yoruba polity rested," and the predominantly male cult, *oro*, with executing justice.[17] Olajubu further points to these functions as a manifestation of power in different realms, the visible realm and the invisible realm, indicating a system of thought in which gender differences are complementary. She notes that in Yoruba symbolism, the male signifies "toughness, volatility, and aggressiveness," while the female signifies a contrasting "coolness, gentleness, and peace." Both are needed for balance, and often in religious practices, prayers call for the presence of both energies. As an illustration of this point, Olajubu cites the following prayer calling for a balancing of energy between the male and female energetic principles during a special festival honoring the orisha Yemonja:

Odun de loni oo
K'Odun ni yi yabo
Abo lala bo mo
Abo ni tura
Abo ni rora
K'Odun wa ma y'ako
Ako lo ni lile

Meaning:
Our festival has arrived today
May this festival turn out to be female in nature.
It is in femaleness that peace is hidden
It is the female that comforts
It is the female that soothes
May our festival not turn out to be male
For toughness is of the male.[18]

Olajubu further points out that all facets of the people's cosmic experiences, as noted in the myths and legends, manifest the principle of gender complementarity, which has a profound bearing on the role of women in Yoruba society.

How do we see this concept of "gender complementarity" played out in contemporary African American Yoruba religious practices? According to the comments of participants in my study, the African American males who are identified by the diviner as having a female guardian orisha, especially those identified as sons of Oshun, have difficulty understanding the concept. Because African American popular culture places great value on "toughness, volatility, and aggressiveness" as male attributes, a young man's being told that he is a child of a female orisha may be a challenge to his manhood. Discussing this phenomenon, one priest commented, "We lost many good priests, especially in the early days, because we were not taught that everyone has a mix of male and female energies. For a man to have a female guardian orisha may simply mean that this is the energy needed to balance out his aggressive, volatile energy."[19]

The priests of Oshun with whom I spoke all indicated that the idea was initially difficult for them to grasp, because they were fearful of being thought of as a "sissy." One priest commented,

> It was a battle for me for awhile being that I'm a man and being that I have a female orisha crowned to my head. For a long time I had problems with that. I didn't accept it, you know, "I'm a man." Then one day this priestess was possessed with Yemonja and she told me, "We all know you're a man. Oshun knows you're a man. So, don't worry about that." It's a different energy. The way I see it Oshun is beauty, but she is also fierce. She's a warrior. People have perceptions of Oshun as being a party animal, the one who likes to dance, the one who likes to party, especially my road which is Ibu Anya. The *bata* drums are made from the anya tree. So people associate my road with the dancing and partying. But my Oshun is tough, at the same time she's sweet. So, being a man and having an Oshun doesn't bother me at all for we all have a masculine and a feminine side. It's about understanding both sides and being able to co-exist. My godmother just made a fourteen-year-old boy who is Oshun and I had to explain to him that it was OK. It's not about sexuality, though people talk about that and they say "Oh, Oshun priests are gay." That's not what it's about at all. My father is Ogun. Ogun is controlled. People think that Ogun is all rough-and-tumble, but my relationship with Ogun is real smooth. He's sharp. He's kind of dirty, but he's real smooth.[20]

Similar comments were made by other African American males initiated to Oshun. For example, a priest of Oshun that I interviewed at Oyotunji Village also commented that he has had a difficult time shaking the "party animal" image. He reported, "If you are a priest of Oshun people automatically think that you love to party, but that is a superficial understanding of what Oshun represents, so I just tried to get an understanding of what the Oshun energy is all about. You know you hear all kinds of things, but I wanted to understand at a deeper level."[21]

Getting to know what an orisha's energy is all about may be a challenge because the system constructed by African American practitioners is still fragmented. One priest remarked, "Many people don't know why they do what they do. They know the rituals, but they don't know the system of thought behind the ritual."[22] Another commented that the cultural psychology is the most important aspect of the tradition because it undergirds everything else, but too often that is the one thing that people do not know about.[23]

The cultural psychology undergirding the popular orisha Oshun and her symbolic representation of fertility, creation, birth, and source of new life is an aje power with a redemptive quality for an enslaved and oppressed people. These qualities are highlighted in the mythological tales cited above. Oshun embodies the aje that makes life sweet, like honey. She represents desire as expressed in sexuality and sensuality. She represents the hope and agency that makes life bearable. In terms of the physical body, Oshun is the blood that runs warm in the veins. All of these constructions of Oshun thus reflect a very powerful feminine energy that is necessary for the creation of human life. An interpretation of Oshun against the Wimbush/Ford paradigm discussed in chapter 2 suggests that she be placed in phase one of the tripartite schema. Phase one, flight or deformation in the Wimbush paradigm and departure in the Ford paradigm, is consistent with Oshun as the deity of birth/beginnings. In Yoruba cosmology, the birth of a child is a departure from the invisible world of spirit and is thus the beginning of a journey along the road of life.

Yemonja

The attributes that form the archetypal energy of the orisha Yemonja in the minds of New World practitioners are the aje of "motherhood." Described as both the punishing mother and the nurturing mother Yemonja represents aspects of life maintenance and day-to-day chores, like cleaning and cooking. Her colors are crystal, light blue, dark blue, coral, and silver, representing the depths of the soul. She is the soul sister, queen of spirits, the spiritualist, and the sixth sense. She loves the black race and is said to have been the spirit that kept enslaved Africans alive during the Middle Passage.[24]

Instructing an introductory class on the Orisha tradition, a New York priest of Obatala described Yemonja as follows:

> Yemonja can be very destructive. She protects and defends her children to death. She's a fierce warrior. She's no joke. When you think of an Amazon or a mother defending her child, that's Yemonja. You can go to her with your problems and she will run interference. She's clairvoyant. Her children receive messages in dreams and premonitions. She likes molasses, pork chops, collard greens, and corn bread. Her numbers are multiples of seven. Her day is Saturday. She is the nurturer, the growth, the caring. A child of Yemonja needs to be trained in certain professions in order to have mental balance. Her children are more prone to be open. Yemonja is the water in the body, the tides that move the ocean. She represents depth. African Americans survived as a people because of her mercy. Yemonja owns the odu Odi.[25]

The nurturing mother, the spiritualist, the soul sister, the one who speaks in dreams, the one who loves and defends black people, the fierce warrior—where do we find her in African American culture? The odu Odi-Osa suggests that she may be found in the caring nature of the mother. The following apataki, part of the Odi corpus, addresses one aspect of the Yemonja energy:

> Like all mothers in the traditional Yoruba culture, it was Yemonja's duty to find a suitable wife for her son Shango. When Yemonja set out to find her son a wife, she immediately thought of the orisha Obba. However, Shango was not too thrilled with his mother's selection. He wanted someone stronger and more fiery to better match his own temperament.
>
> The orisha Oya would have been perfect for him, as she was a strong and fiery woman and also enchantingly beautiful. Unfortunately, she was the wife of Ogun, the god of war. Ogun was always

absorbed in campaigning or hunting, and never paid much attention to his beautiful wife.

One day, while Ogun was on a hunting expedition, Oya went to the marketplace. On her way she passed the palace where Shango happened to be holding a festival. He danced with grace and undeniable power. When she laid eyes on him she was immediately spellbound. Oya could not get the handsome dancer out of her mind. When time came for another festival, she decided to bring him a gift of cola nuts, which was a mistake, because regular cola nuts were one of his taboo foods. To be offered his taboo was a great insult.

Yemonja had seen the whole thing. She had especially noted the look in her son's eyes when he first saw Oya. Immediately she stepped in, calming Shango's volatile temper and defending Oya. Oya returned with fine bitter cola nuts and made the proper offering to Shango. The two looked into each other's eyes and were smitten. Shango asked Oya to marry him. Concealing the fact that she was already married to Ogun, she agreed. Over the next several weeks, the preparations were made, and the two were wed.

When Ogun finally returned from his hunting expedition, he heard the news of the marriage and was outraged. He rushed to the palace and challenged Shango to do battle. They fought an all-out war that shook the pillars of heaven.

To find a solution, Obatala called them into a council of the orisha. He presented them with a riddle. Whoever came up with the correct answer would keep Oya as his own. They were each charged to bring Obatala a sample of outside cotton and inside cotton. Yemonja consulted with Elegbara, who told Shango that inside cotton was a spider's web, and outside cotton was grown in a field. When the day came, Shango won the contest, and Oya was given to him as his wife.

But there was still the matter of Obba. She had left her home and now was disgraced by Shango's rejection. In her despair she felt that she could never return home, so she used her magic to turn herself into a river. Yemonja told Shango that because of what he had done to Obba, Oya might be his wife, but she could never bear children for him.[26]

This apataki focuses on Yemonja as the caring mother, making every effort to provide her offspring with what would make him happy in life. She is also one who seeks justice and fairness, making it clear that every action has its own consequences. Among African American practitioners, Yemonja is credited with the energy of survival and perseverance during the Middle Passage and the time of enslavement. She is seen as the nurturing mother that one can always depend upon in a time of need.

Omo Yemonja (children of, i.e., those initiated to Yemonja) speak of this energy matrix in varied ways.

> We are drama queens. Every child of Yemonja must have drama.[27]

> Daughters of Yemonja love children. I always wanted lots of children, even before I knew that Yemonja was my guardian orisha. I had several miscarriages and eventually adopted five children. Yemonja had already told me that I would have many children, but give birth to none. I did not believe her, but she was right.[28]

> I am a priest of Yemonja and any of my godchildren will tell you that I am a compassionate and nurturing godfather.[29]

> I love being a mother. I have six children. I love nature. I talk to the plants, the flowers and trees in my yard. Later I learned that Yemonja is considered the mother of the plant kingdom and the animal kingdom. I feel very close to nature. I own a business making and selling garments that I tie-dye. Many of the designs that I use I created without even knowing they were almost identical to some of the traditional African designs. It was much later that I found out that the art of tie-dyeing belongs to Yemonja. It came to me through inheritance and I don't know how many generations back. The odu Irosun speaks of inheritance, and that odu was very prevalent throughout my ita. It even came up in the reading that said it was time for me to be initiated.[30]

> I'm a spiritualist and I always have been, but I did not recognize my powers. From childhood I have dreamed of things that actually happened.[31]

These comments reflect the nurturing mother, the spiritualist, and the drama queen, common motifs in the conversations of female adherents. The following story describes a priestess of Yemonja in trance possession (an altered state of consciousness in which a practitioner assumes the identity of an orisha) and gives another example of the Yemonja energy in active engagement:

> Once at a *bembe* there were about sixty people in my driveway dancing for hours, and I watched a priestess of Yemonja dance into possession. After a while she began to "swim" through the crowd, and one by one she began to pull people from the crowd and take them over to the side and direct them to lie down on the ground. Then she lay on top of each one. Afterwards she got up and took a piece of blue cloth and prayed into it and swept it over each person. When all of this was over, I interviewed each person and they all made similar comments, saying that emotional issues had come up for them and they felt like Yemonja had pulled them out and had saved them from drowning in their emotions. She had cleaned them by sweeping the blue cloth over them and they felt refreshed and renewed as a result. A few days after that I heard a news report about a number of whales "beaching" themselves because the waters were not safe. This is what Yemonja did for those practitioners. She did it through the sacred dance of the priestess who channeled the Yemonja energy. Sacred dance changes the energy field and opens one to receive messages that are constantly being broadcast from the universe. The information could be for an individual, for the world, or for the cosmos.[32]

Here we see the manifestation of a healing and nurturing aje power. In this scene, the Yemonja priestess in possession is a channel of communication with the divine. She enters into this altered state of consciousness after dancing before the drums. In her discussion of the significance of dance in the Yoruba tradition, Luisah Teish, a priestess of Oshun, comments that dance is a ritual offering that transforms the dancer and serves as an entry into the spirit world, that dance is a medicine as well as a mystery. It is a ritual enactment of myth that bridges the worlds of the past and the present, the physical and the spiritual. In her words, "Dance is a meditation of the body, an extrovert meditation that changes the psychic field." When asked if there is a yoga of breath in the African tradition, she answers that it is in the dance. When asked if there is an African book of prayer, she answers, "It's in the song, the dance, the drum, in the movement of everyday life. It does not live on the page. It is in the dance."[33]

From her research work on ceremonial spirit possession, psychologist Sheila S. Walker concludes that possession is a complex phenomenon marked by neurophysiological changes frequently produced by sensory bombardment in the form of the "sonic driving of the drum rhythms." She suggests that the people dancing, singing, and moving together in close proximity in a ceremonial atmosphere in which possession is expected also add to the vibrational impact of the drum. Walker also notes that "it is ultimately the belief system and values of the society which determine the existence, nature, and psycho-social function of the complex altered state of consciousness known in folk theory as possession."[34]

Luisah Teish's report of her conversation with participants in the scenario described above is consistent with Walker's observations. Those who were "beached" by Yemonja were practitioners who embraced a system of belief that included the possibility and probability of a deity communicating through the body of an individual in such settings. Each participant reported positive value in the experience, i.e., they felt as though they had been rescued from a sea of drowning emotions. Teish asserts that the phenomenon of ceremonial possession stands out as a common thread among orisha worshippers throughout the African Diaspora. According to her, "a devotee, whether she is at a ceremony in Nigeria, Brazil, or Cuba can become possessed by a deity, and her behavior will be in accordance with the prescribed behavior of that deity in Africa."[35]

Through her poetic words, Luisah Teish constructs yet another image of Yemonja:

> Gaze upon the waters of Yemaya for your own self's sake. Perform rituals on the ocean at sunrise and midnight for your healing. Watch Her shimmering in the light of the full moon and be renewed. There is no mountain of trouble that Yemaya cannot wear down; no sickness of heart that She cannot wash clean; no desert of despair that She cannot flood with hope.
>
> Come, my sisters, embrace Her! Feel her spray on your face! Inhale her mist! Power is the name of Yemaya-Olokun.[36]

The healing/personal empowerment theme is also echoed in the following original tale included in Teish's description of Yemonja:

> Once there was a beautiful woman by the name of Ye-ma-ya, who looked into the waters of the ocean. There She saw Her own reflection and asked, "Who is that beautiful woman? I thought that I was the prettiest thing that the World had ever seen!"

And as She looked on that woman there came a rumbling in Her belly and it grew and it grew and it grew until it exploded and covered the land with lakes, rivers, and streams.

Yemaya looked into the water of the river and there again She saw that woman and asked, "Who is that beautiful woman? I thought that I was the prettiest thing that the World had ever seen!"

And again Her belly grew and it grew and it grew till it exploded and sprinkled the heavens with stars and a full moon.

Yemanja looked in the full moon, and again she asked, "Who is that beautiful woman? I thought that I was the prettiest thing that the world had ever seen!"

And again Her belly grew, and it grew and it grew until it exploded! And before Her stood thousands of beautiful women.

Yemaya asked, "Who are you beautiful women? I thought that I was the prettiest thing that the world had ever seen!"

The women looked deep into the Eyes of Yemaya and there they saw their own reflections.

So the women said to Yemaya, "You are! We're just you!"[37]

This story, included in Teish's book of personal charms and practical rituals, functions as a tool of self-empowerment by focusing on Yemonja as a representation of inner power, beauty, and creative force. Prescriptive in nature, this tale urges the practitioner to see self as reflected in nature, to gaze upon this reflection, and to be renewed. Here Yemonja represents a healing/personal empowerment form of aje as an aspect of the archetypal caring mother.

Practitioners say that Oshun gives birth to the child, but Yemonja raises the child. Yemonja represents the water in the physical body and is thus a feminine energy that is necessary for the maintenance of life. In the Wimbush/Ford social formation paradigm, Yemonja relates to phase two—building or formation in the Wimbush schema, and fulfillment in the Ford schema. Some of the symbols of Yemonja—the (controversial) black mammy doll and the common soul-food dishes of collard greens, corn bread, molasses, and watermelon as ritual foods—reflect the nature of her construction as the comforting, caring mother. The fact that she is given credit for the survival of Africans during the Middle Passage and the subsequent period of enslavement in the United States indicates that practitioners give credence to an indispensable feminine power.

Oya

African American constructions of the orisha Oya depict her as radical change. As Oshun represents birth, Oya represents death, whether physical or metaphorical. The following notes from a discussion group hosted by a priest of Oya in Brooklyn, New York, give a detailed picture of the energy matrix known as Oya:

> Oya comes from Nupe country out of Nigeria . . . out of the Niger River flowing from North into Yorubaland. Oya is the weather goddess. She is in thunder, lightning, fire, and wind. When hot air mixes with low cool air to give hurricanes, Oya is cleaning the air. Her number is nine. Her colors are done in sets of nine or multicolor—purple, brown, crimson red. In Nigeria she is the marketplace. In this country, the cemetery and the marketplace, but more emphasis is placed on the cemetery. Her emblems are the machete, black horsetail, flamboyant tree with long seeded pods. She is the warrior orisha who fought with Shango. Shango had many wives. Oya was the last and was faithful. She was also the wife of Ogun (god of war). In living with Ogun she stole his war properties. So she has the same emblems as Ogun. As orisha of the cemetery, she is highly connected with the *egungun* (society for the veneration of ancestors).
>
> She is the only female who can get inside the men's society of *egungun*. She knows the secrets of the masqueraders. In Cuba, Oya takes on the same attributes, but comes out with face masks. Oya has many different faces. As she goes into battle her face changes. No one wants to look at her face when she's angry so she's sometimes masked. She is represented by the pinwheel, the turning of air.
>
> Oya is the orisha of the edges, boundaries. For example, air coming into contact with land. Oya means "to tear." As Oya comes in contact with land she rips whatever is in her path. Through her floodwaters the land gets ripped open. In ceremonies for her, cloth is ripped apart. The ripping effect gives change. Oya is very fiery. Her foods are dark-colored fruits (black grapes, red grapes, black plums), eggplants, animals—she-goats, black fowls, and guinea hens. Her *elekes* are red, brown, black and white stripes.
>
> She has a close relationship with Shango. Shango controls the thunderbolt. Oya controls the lightning. A clap of thunder is said to be the mating of the two. The story has it that Shango was always getting

into trouble. He once decided to steal some stuff from a *babalu* and got locked up. The flies came and told Oya. She changed Shango into a fly, and he was able to escape.

Oya is a fighter, but she is compassionate and merciful. Once her mind is made up she is very unyielding. She is the orisha of change and transformation, going from one point to another.

Oya is the epitome of class. She serves things in a special way. If you ask for water, she puts it in a goblet. She announces things with style, even when she's going to kill you. She'll say, "You got nine days to get it together." I saw this happen. The godchildren begged and pleaded for the man's life, but she said, "No. You need not bother. I'm taking him in nine days." In nine days he was dead. Oya is the goddess of death, living at the edge of the cemetery.

Oya represents the cutting edge, the pioneer. Before you know there is a way, Oya is there. She's a trendsetter. Oya cleans us and transforms us. When her beads are presented, cloth is ripped to represent the process of rebirth. Oya is multidimensional; the concept of one thing ending, another beginning. The stages of maturation characterize her unique form of aje power. Each stage is a metamorphosis or death.

Oya controls the respiratory system—colds, bronchitis, asthma, winds and movement of air. The Yoruba looked at death as change. Each stage brings on something else. Oya hides behind Osumare (the rainbow), the many colors. Even men who are initiated to Oya have an Oya skirt. The skirt is worn in ceremony by both male and female. In the early years of initiation in this country men did not understand why they were initiated to a female orisha. A lot of good priests were lost because they were not able to incorporate that concept. This was a problem for African American males.[38]

The theme of change is paramount in the above discussion of the characteristics of Oya. One diviner reported that during the height of the Black Consciousness movement in the 1960s and '70s, a number of college students were read as omo Oya (children of Oya).[39] He explained that since this was a time of radical social change in America, it was not surprising that Oya, the orisha of change, would have a noticeable presence.

Oya controls the odu Osa, an odu that "represents the destructive side of nature, the forces that cause one quality to mutate into its opposite."[40] The dualistic symbolism of the odu Osa is very similar to the parent sign, Odi.

Both represent opposing forces, but while Odi uses opposing forces to create something new and seal it, Osa destroys the seal and deconstructs the thing that has been created, turning it back into its component parts, creating new potential and possibility.[41] The following original tale by Luisah Teish reflects her personal experience with this energy matrix:

> Whirling Wind was the one who cast Ifa for Nine Skirts on the day She heard the cry, "Help, Oya, help me to change."
>
> The human held to pain and said, "My head is dizzy with ugly thoughts, my belly is hard with greed, my knees are weak with the weight of guilt, and the leaves will not cure me."
>
> Oya spun around on Her toes.
>
> The human cried, "What must I do for you, Oya, what is your price for my cure?"
>
> Oya spun around on Her fingers.
>
> "Must I give you all my gold? Must I surrender my ego? Shall I beg your forgiveness?"
>
> Oya spun around on Her head.
>
> The human screamed and cried, "Please, Twirling Woman. Help me. Help me!"
>
> Oya flashed Her dark mirror and said, "If you wish release, Human, simply look into my mirror and change. You who need courage . . . look into my mirror and change. If you desire wisdom, simply . . . look into my mirror and change. Power can be yours if you will . . . look into my mirror and change."
>
> And so the human looked into Her mirror and changed!
>
> "Oh, Oya, my head is clear, my belly . . . soft, my knees are strong! What must I do to pay you for this wonder?"
>
> Oya took a wide-legged step and She fanned Her skirts just so. And all the curing leaves fell from the trees and laid a path before the human.
>
> Whirling Wind was the one who cast Ifa for Nine Skirts on the day She heard the cry.
>
> Oya smiled and said, "You who seek transformation need only look into my mirror . . . and *change*!"[42]

Teish situates her work in the "Woman Spirit Movement." This is also a demonstration of aje power.[43] Casting Oya as a whirlwind, this story speaks of an energy matrix that serves as a catalyst for healing, personal power, and self-transformation. It is part of Teish's arsenal of stories, amulets, rituals, and talismans for courage, wisdom, and power for constructing and reconstructing self and world.

Without any knowledge of its association with the Yoruba orisha Oya, the metaphor of the whirlwind has appeared in African American history as a symbol for change since the early twentieth century, if not earlier. In 1925, Marcus Garvey, now best remembered as a champion of the Back-to-Africa movement, wrote these words from prison: "Look for me in the whirlwind or the storm, look for me all around you, for, with God's grace, I shall come and bring with me countless millions of black slaves who have died in America and the West Indies and the millions in Africa to aid you in the fight for Liberty, Freedom and Life."[44] The collective autobiography of the "New York 21"—the twenty-one members of the Black Panther Party who were arrested in 1969 for "crimes against society"—takes its title, *Look for Me in the Whirlwind*, from this quotation. The whirlwind metaphor, as used here, represents an unyielding commitment to radical social change. Why the whirlwind metaphor? A "whirlwind" is defined as a small mass of air rotating rapidly in a spiral, or a rapidly moving, destructive force that is like a whirlwind or tornado.[45] Perhaps, then, both Marcus Garvey in 1925 and the Black Panthers in 1969 chose to represent themselves as a whirlwind because they understood themselves to be small in mass, yet powerful in force, set on destroying social injustice. In the oracular imagination of the Orisha tradition, this would be the work of Oya. As Judith Gleason explains it, *O-ya* in Yoruba means "She tore." "She tore and a huge tree was ripped from its roots. She tore. A river overflowed its banks. Barriers were broken down."[46] Luisah Teish refers to Oya as the "Goddess of the Winds of Change. . . . the dutiful Mother of Catastrophe, the one who destroys outworn structures and sweeps away debris."[47] The archetypal Oya energy thus reflects an aje power that is a critical part of the cycle of life. She stands before the gateway of death, the last threshold and passageway before rebirth. In the Wimbush/Ford paradigms, Oya represents the third and final phase—"reformulation" in Wimbush's schema, and "return" in Ford's. In Yoruba cosmology, Oya represents the reformulation that takes place in the return to the spirit world, the completion of the cycle of life. She also represents the marketplace, the place where many transactions are completed.

As noted in the preceding discussion, African American constructions of Oya reflect the boundaries, the edge, the cutting edge, the pioneer, radical change, the winds that cast off the old to make way for the new. Oya, then, reflects an aspect of the archetypal mother that is just as important and as powerful as Oshun and Yemonja. She is the air of the respiratory system, another function essential to life. She, Oshun, and Yemonja are elaborating symbols that help explain critical passages along the journey of life.

CONCLUSION

Over the course of this study, I not only examined African American engagements with Yoruba scriptures but also began to situate my work in conversation with questions posed by the Institute for Signifying Scriptures at Claremont Graduate University. I considered the significance of broader orientations to scriptures and the psychosocial and cultural needs addressed through their engagement.[1] In the Yoruba worldview, the oracle—accessed primarily through the divination ritual—serves as a source of guidance on all major life decisions and provides the basis for understanding one's self in relationship to the world. The Orisha tradition grew in popularity in America during a time of black nationalism and separatist ideology; its West African roots added to its appeal for African Americans. So, too, did its emphasis on exercising agency in changing one's life. The Odu as scripture represents a set of principles that are dynamic, active, and performative, constantly in motion, creating, generating, re-creating, and altering human experience.

But how I have learned is just as important as what I have learned, for it is the how, in addition to the what, that has significant implications for future epistemologies and pedagogies in the field of religious studies. I learned by leaving the familiar and venturing out to explore the unknown through walks around the streets of Harlem, subway rides to other boroughs—Brooklyn, the Bronx, Queens—as well as plane trips to Savannah and road trips to Sheldon, South Carolina. I learned by talking with and listening to practitioners who came from North Carolina, South Carolina, New York, Philadelphia, Chicago, Georgia, and Florida to attend Orisha festivals at Oyotunji African Village in Sheldon. I engaged all of my senses, and some of those sensory experiences have lingered in my memory. The Beads, Body, and Soul exhibit at the Studio Museum of Harlem on 125th Street gave me a glimpse of the aesthetic power of artfully constructed orisha altars. The Metropolitan Museum of Art's exhibit Art and Oracle: Spirit Voices of Africa taught me what Rowland Abiodun meant when he said that the orisha Ela was the first to speak, speaking through the creative power of the artist. I was dazzled by the evocative power of the divination artifacts on display, the strikingly beautiful, exquisitely beaded, and intricately carved ritual objects and ceremonial masks that spoke volumes about the imaginative expression of a sacred worldview in the Yoruba culture.

The Caribbean Cultural Center's Saturday workshop called The Altar of My Soul, based on Marta Vega's popular book of the same title, brought me face-to-face with women of all ages seeking a community of understanding where they could explore the meaning of dreams, spirit visitations, and divinatory readings. By listening deeply, seeing with new eyes, and singing, dancing, touching, tasting, and smelling, I came to know something of what practitioners mean when they speak of *awo* as a form of knowledge that must be experienced and cannot be known by the intellect alone. It was not only by my focus on the people—what I observed of their interactions with the Odu, along with the stories they shared—but also by my participation, interaction, and reflections that I learned of the significance of the Odu as the voice of the gods in the lives of African American Ifa/Orisha practitioners. Through my study of the lives of practitioners, I learned about inner and outer signifying places and spaces. I concluded that such spaces and places are intricately connected to scripturalizing practices. And scripturalizing practices often serve to indicate the practitioner's major concerns, attitudes, and actions at a given point in time. Signifying spaces and places can be inner temperaments or emotional states like anger, fear, anxiety, pain, joy, uncertainty, depression, creativity, silence, and awareness. They can also be exterior conditions and material locations of meaning, such as altars, temples, shrines, the divining mat, the *bembe*, the ritual, and the ceremony. Such spaces and places represent, reflect, and provide information about the client's personal and social state of being, often in coded form.

They come into play when the researcher shifts the focus from the conventional text of a written scripture to the people and their engagements with scriptures. The life story interview was one of the means by which I studied individual lives and their personal history of engagement with scriptures. As Herbert Rubin and Irene Rubin have explained, such qualitative interviews operate like "night-vision goggles, permitting us to see that which is not ordinarily on view and examine that which is often looked at but seldom seen."[2] The life story interview performs in this way, providing a window that opens onto the interior life of the individual in social context.

Study of Lives

Psychologists examine life stories in an effort to understand human development and personality; anthropologists, to study aspects of culture; sociologists, to study social interaction; and educators, to teach. In a similar vein, scholars of religion use the life story to study how individuals and communities narrate the experience and symbol of God. What can the scholar of religion learn about scriptures from the study of lives through the life story interview? By listening to and examining the personal narrative, we can identify and come to know the unique way in which the individual has expressed and lived out the human story, for "our personal story, at its essence, is the human story."[3] Robert Atkinson, a human development psychologist and director of the University of Southern Maine's Center for the Study of Lives, argues that personal myths share a common sacred pattern, the same pattern that can be seen in the stories that we set aside, assign power and authority to and designate as scripture. This classic tripartite pattern may be expressed as beginning, "muddle," resolution; birth, death, rebirth; challenge, choice, outcome; separation, initiation, return; or flight, formation, reformulation. This pattern appears over and over in individual stories as well as in myth, folktales, and other sacred narratives.

Through in-depth life story interviews, I have drawn from the voices of the people by listening to their stories, participating in their rituals and ceremonies, and documenting their lives. I have seen how the Odu functions as a body of sacred stories that connects the individual story of self with a greater human story. Is this not what scriptures do? When individuals and communities engage scriptures, they find personal resonance that links their experience of a situation, circumstance, or feeling with a parallel human experience. Ifa divination functions both as a compass and as a navigation system, helping clients locate themselves and map their lives. When the diviner interprets the Odu, he or she tells a story and then helps clients identify themselves in the story. For example, a client of one babalawo told me that he said she was "the shining bird in the story." When I asked, "What was the story?," she responded, "Oh, I didn't think to ask what the story was." In this instance, the client had been given a metaphor that helped her see herself in a new light. She told me that in a follow-up conversation, she had learned that the story associated with the odu of her divination session was about a bird that encountered many challenges and difficulties, but in the end came out shining. "Whenever I feel discouraged and want to give up," she said, "I remember that I am the shining bird and that gives me hope so that I am able to keep going." This example illustrates one of the functions of scriptures. Scriptures may provide a parallel image of the self that inspires, provides hope, and helps a person navigate the vicissitudes of life. Scriptures, because of the power assigned to them, are powerful motivators of action, positive and negative.

The life story interview as a methodology allows the scholar of religion to see how the individual engages sacred story and how the sacred pattern plays out in the individual life. By examining and comparing life story data, researchers become aware of the range of scripturalizing practices in the life of a community or in the life of an individual over time. When individuals tell their life stories to the researcher, they speak of those experiences, thoughts, feelings, actions, and events that have affected them most, thereby revealing the way in which they see and experience life. Life stories speak of the journey of the soul, and through the emotive quality of the story, individuals connect with each other across barriers of time and tradition. Atkinson writes, "Stories—those that have been told across the generations, as well as our own—inform, inspire, teach, maintain moral codes, record events that become history, establish family lines and genealogy, preserve customs, guide us, show us possibilities, open our hearts, make us laugh, and clarify all aspects of life while healing and transforming. We are, all of us, living stories, eager to find our own voices by which we can be known to others."[4] Perhaps this is another function of scripture, providing the larger human blueprint with which individuals can connect their lives and find their own voices.

With every interview, I struggled to capture more than a talking head, but a whole person in social context with both an inner and an outer life. Chief Ajamu, the first diviner I interviewed, loved a captive audience and was a great storyteller. He told me stories about growing up in Chicago in the Catholic Church, attending Catholic schools, and learning about the spirit world from his grandmother at a young age. He was born with a veil in 1940 and always had second sight, but he had difficulty applying his intuitive wisdom to his own life. He wanted to be a Catholic priest when he grew up, but fate had other plans. By his early twenties he had two children and an ex-wife. For a while he attended college and worked as a community organizer in the civil rights movement. He later dropped out of college and held a variety of odd jobs. At the time of his introduction to Ifa, he was unemployed. His life was in shambles. One day he was hanging out with some friends, and someone told him that they had heard about a man in Africa, a babalawo, who could help you get your life straightened out. He followed up and sent a letter with a couple of dollars to this man in Africa. After about a month he received a letter in response. This man, whom he had never seen or talked to, told him astounding things about his life, things that even his friends didn't know. This divinatory reading, this message from the gods, was the beginning of the road that led to Ifa. I don't know what his name was at that time, but this young man, who later was to become Chief Ajamu, was about to rewrite his story. By asking around he found out about a Yoruba temple in Chicago, and he made his way to it. There he learned that a priest in New York was planning to start an African village in South Carolina. This was all he needed to know. He traveled to South Carolina and became part of the founding of Oyotunji African Village in 1970. A few years later, he was initiated into the priesthood and became a diviner.

I met Chief Ajamu in 1999. The above account comes from his narration of his story. It follows the classic tripartite structure of challenge, choice, and outcome. He was what performance ethnographers call a reader of worlds, individual and social worlds. Through the study of his life and the lives of other diviners, I came to know performance ethnography as the difference between "reading the word" and "reading the world." As educator Joan Wink explains it, when we read words, we bring ourselves to the pages to interpret meaning, but when we read worlds, it is somewhat different: we are then assessing the people and community around us, including visible and invisible messages.[5]

Wink, paraphrasing Paulo Freire and Donaldo Macedo's *Literacy: Reading the Word and the World*, further points out that traditionally, literacy has been thought of in terms of reading the word, but she calls for a critical literacy that equips one to read the visible and invisible messages of the world. Following this line of thought, then, it is the invention and engagement of "scriptures"—the *doing* (the performance, the enactment, the construction, the motion)—that provides scholars of religion a broader, more textured site of investigation than the *done* (the text). Denzin, drawing from the work of Conquergood and Schechner, highlights five elements for consideration that are consistent with Wink's perspective on "reading the world." These elements include performance and cultural process, ethnographic praxis, hermeneutics, scholarly representation, and the politics of culture.[6]

Focusing on "reading the world" has implications for the study of "scriptures." Chief Ajamu often objected to the use of the word "religion," insisting that the word "culture" was a more accurate description of the Ifa/Orisha tradition. Culture is an ongoing performance, a process in the center of the lived experience. To think of "scriptures" in the context of performance and cultural process is to think of dynamic interaction. When the Yoruba diviner speaks of the "odu that fell," we think of an active process, something in motion, something happening, something beyond the scope of text. Performance and ethnographic praxis highlights fieldwork as a collaborative process. The "participant observer" is a co-performer, a co-creator and collaborator in the construction of knowledge: "Performance and hermeneutics . . . privileges experience as a way of knowing, a method of critical inquiry, and as a mode of understanding."[7] In the Yoruba tradition, Esu is the god of interpretation, representing, among other things, irony, fluidity, and in-determinacy. A collaborator in the construction of knowledge, with the guidance of a practitioner, I wrote the following *oriki* to Esu as an appropriate metaphor for the study of scripture as both text and performance:

> Esu, the trickster, the one who can stand in two opposing camps and feel no shame . . .
> Esu, the one who walks with a limp because he has one foot planted firmly in each of two worlds, the world of the human and the world of the divine
> Esu, the Divine Messenger
> Esu, the God of Interpretation
> Esu, the one with two faces, the guardian of the cross roads
> Esu, the capricious child, and the wise elder
> Esu, the principle of multi-vocality, double-voiced utterance, and indeterminacy[8]

The insights from the Yoruba god of interpretation suggest that the scholar of religion who practices a critical pedagogy develops strategies for close-up viewing and analysis of scripture as a production site, a site where meaning and power are produced. Denzin's analysis of performance, the act of scholarly representation, and the politics of culture raises questions about treating "performance as a complementary form of research publication, an alternative method or way of interpreting and presenting the results of an ethnographer's work."[9] Denzin argues that a performance authorizes itself, and by evoking shared experiences, it becomes a way of connecting the biographical, the pedagogical, and the political.[10] Borrowing the phrase "creative analytical practices" from Laurel Richardson, he notes that performance narrative forms are many and varied, including fiction, short stories, personal narratives, photographic essays, dialogue, creative nonfiction, drama, and fragmented or layered text—all ways in which the writer is self-consciously present in the reporting. This area was one of great challenge to me. I wanted to be self-consciously present in the reporting, but I wasn't quite sure how to proceed. I combed the literature on the performance model as critical pedagogy, looking for clues on how to produce a book that acknowledged my experiential presence and creatively provided space for the direct speech of the practitioners to take center stage. I found educational theorist Randall Hill's work on the value of the performance pedagogical model helpful. Hill posits that the performance model improves one's understanding of the relationship between the investigator and the investigated because it depends on both analytical and experiential ways of knowing. Moreover, it is based on a "collaborative learning model that does not value one voice above another."[11]

Other educators, too, have shared the results of using the performance model as pedagogical praxis. Carol L. Benton, for example, reports that she has been amazed by the positive responses of students who were taught to use a performance model in an introductory course in women's studies. In spite of the anxiety students initially expressed about their assignment, in the end, they claimed that it was the most powerful and meaningful aspect of the class. The projects took on a life of their own.[12] Benton's students crafted dramatic readings, dialogues, and narratives based on their explorations of women's issues. This proved to be an engaging form of learning, one that had a great impact on the students.

New Testament scholar Musa Dube notes that at one point, she literally stopped in her tracks when she realized that her teaching approaches had little to do with the pain and suffering in the lives of her students, many of whom were affected by the HIV-AIDS epidemic in Africa. It was at this point that she decided to select biblical texts on "healing" and have her students go into the field and ask people in the communities to read those texts and talk about them in relationship to the AIDS epidemic. Students then returned to the classroom and told the stories they had heard. This exercise shifted the focus from the text to the people in relationship to the text, and out of it grew a new focus for what Paulo Freire refers to as a "pedagogy of hope."[13] It provided a new arena within which students could construct and represent knowledge. It also fueled Dube's focus on socially engaged, community-based scholarship. Dube frequently presents her research in a storytelling performance that weaves cultural tales, biblical texts, and contemporary social issues into a dramatic rendition of song and spoken word that is extremely powerful and compelling.[14]

Each of the above examples speaks to the value of a performance model for critical pedagogy. By shifting the focus from "texts" to "worlds" in the study of Yoruba "scriptures" in African American culture, I also embrace the value of ethnography and performance theory to the study of "scriptures." Such approaches, by focusing on the people and their production of "scriptures" as a way of finding order and meaning in life, provide agency to those whose voices may otherwise be mute. That said, it is difficult to imagine how to write a book that would capture the power and dynamism expressed by people narrating their experiences with the Odu within the conventions of a scholarly discipline. I briefly considered applying lessons from Karen McCarthy Brown's *Mama Lola: A Vodou Priestess in Brooklyn*—an artful use of fiction, creative nonfiction, and analytical observations that transports the reader to the center of a family's religious life—or from Paul Stollar's rich narrative, *In Sorcery's Shadow: A Memoir of Apprenticeship Among the Songhay of Niger.* I ultimately resolved, though, that I would rely on descriptive ethnographic scenes, interview passages, and reflexive analytical commentary. I found that paying attention to the direct speech of the individuals as they narrated their experiences revealed the significance of the life story as a primary source for studying scripturalizing practices and their significance in the lives of individuals and communities of practitioners.

This approach is consistent with womanist scholar Katie Cannon's insistence that personal narratives and anecdotal evidence must be taken seriously in our efforts to construct knowledge that is based on the theoretical issues born of our living.[15] Those issues include how African Americans narrate the experience and symbol of God, the personal mythmaking approaches used in the movement from personal narrative to universal story. Their narrations included the conjured spaces of divination and inner and outer signifying spaces. By "conjured spaces," I mean those spaces that are designated for special purposes of generative, creative dialogue and interaction. When the diviner spreads a mat on the floor and invites the client to join him or her there, a signifying space has been created, a place filled with symbolic meanings communicated through objects, gestures, sounds, and colors.

Material Culture

It was only after reviewing my field notes several times that I realized the important role of material culture to the process of engaging Yoruba scriptures. My initial focus was on the storied environment, but I later realized that the material culture of visual, embodied, sensory stimuli is an important aspect of the construction of knowledge and self-understanding for the practitioner. The emphasis is on communicating with and drawing wisdom from the invisible world of spirit to help address the immediate concerns of the client. Important ritual objects, as well as spaces, sensations, and performances, are involved in the process, and each makes a significant contribution to the divinatory construction of knowledge. Reflecting on the divination sessions that I observed as well as those in which I participated brings to mind the significance of material culture to communication with the gods.

The most obvious material symbol, the divining board, serves as a visual metaphor for the universe. The iconic image of Esu, the god of interpretation, communication, and point of convergence, strategically carved at the top center of the border and surrounded by images from the animal and human kingdoms, speaks to an understanding of self as intimately connected to and influenced by forces from the visible physical world and invisible spirit world. The diviner's emblematic odu markings in the fine *irosun* powder sprinkled on the divining board speaks to the individual's performance in the world. The divining board represents the world, and the emblematic markings of the odu serve as an index to the mythic link between the socially situated story of the individual and a larger human story. The board becomes a symbol of the ground on which the scripture materializes in human form. The client, then, is an actor in the drama of human history. The diviner's ritual objects—the tapper for rhythmic chanting to open the portal to a field of wisdom and knowledge beyond the physical world, the divining chain, the palm nuts, the cowrie shells—are all material objects that have been consecrated for spirit work, imbued with spirit power and designated for ritual use in reading the script that is viewed as the sacred dispensation from the gods.

Focusing on the Odu in performative terms fills a gap in the existing literature. Previous works have discussed the Odu from a literary or ethical perspective. This study also confirms the relationality of "scripture" and demonstrates important methodological tools for a relational approach to the study of "scriptures" in the lived religious experience. It suggests that "scriptures" are very much like the Yoruba god Esu—that is, fluid, elusive, double-voiced, and multifaceted. It raises important epistemological and pedagogical issues about how knowledge is constructed and how religion is taught. The act of studying the diviners at work, consulting the oracle, producing a narrative, and offering scriptural interpretations, is to examine an alternative way of knowing. The use of a performance paradigm, for instance, calls attention to music, dance, movement, activity, and action, change, adaptation, cultural production, power dynamics, interactions, and so on.

The broader implications of my study, then, center on the possibilities for developing a road map for scholars of religion interested in engaging students in this active learning process of the study of religion and the study of scriptures—the process of constructing knowledge from the borderlands. As I experiment with these ideas in my undergraduate teaching, I recognize the need for the textbook on technique, only to realize that it has not yet been written.

NOTES

Introduction

1. Kola Abimbola, *Yoruba Culture: A Philosophical Account* (Birmingham, U.K.: Iroko Academic Publishers, 2006), 35.

2. Stephen Prothero, *God Is Not One: The Eight Rival Religions That Run the World and Why Their Differences Matter* (New York: HarperCollins, 2010).

3. Albert J. Raboteau, *Slave Religion: The "Invisible Institution" in the Antebellum South,* updated ed. (New York: Oxford University Press, 2004), 7–8.

4. The Institute for Signifying Scriptures, a research center directed by Vincent L. Wimbush and housed at Claremont Graduate University in Claremont, California, sponsors conferences and forums to discuss this approach to the study of scriptures. See http://www.signifyingscriptures.org.

5. Dwight Conquergood, "Beyond the Texts: Toward a Performative Cultural Politics," in *The Future of Performance Studies: Visions and Revisions,* ed. Sheron J. Dailey (Annandale, Va.: National Communication Association, 1998), 26.

6. Ibid.

7. Norman K. Denzin, "The Call to Performance," *Symbolic Interaction* 26, no. 1 (2003): 187–207.

8. From Vincent L. Wimbush's unpublished paper, "Scriptures: Fathoming a Complex Social-Cultural Phenomenon," presented at Theorizing Scriptures, the international conference held February 27–28, 2004, at Claremont Graduate University. The conference launched the Institute for Signifying Scriptures.

9. Joseph R. Roach, *Cities of the Dead: Circum-Atlantic Performance* (New York: Columbia University Press, 1996), 11.

10. Robert W. Preucel, *Archaeological Semiotics* (Malden, Mass.: Wiley-Blackwell, 2010), 66. Preucel provides a concise summary of Peirce's ideas regarding signs. He also compares two schools of thought—one associated with Peirce and the other with Ferdinand de Saussure. The Saussurean school focused on linguistics and the study of languages, while Peirce added a distinctive twist through a focus on pragmatism, or the theory that meanings are determined by considering the practical consequences of ideas or actions.

11. Ibid., 56.

12. Sherry B. Ortner, "On Key Symbols," *American Anthropologist* 75 (1973): 1338–46, reprinted in *A Reader in the Anthropology of Religion,* ed. Michael Lambek (Malden, Mass.: Blackwell, 2002), 159–67.

13. Henry Louis Gates Jr., "A Myth of Origins: Esu-Elegbara and the Signifying Monkey," in *African Intellectual Heritage: A Book of Sources,* ed. Molefi Kete Asante and Abu S. Abarry (Philadelphia: Temple University Press, 1996), 160–75. See also *The Signifying Monkey: A Theory of African-American Literary Criticism* (New York: Oxford University Press, 1988).

14. Afolabi A. Epega and Philip John Neimark, *The Sacred Ifa Oracle* (Brooklyn, N.Y.: Athelia Henrietta Press, 1995), 123. This odu is also the signature for Obatala and Oshun, both of whom are considered guardian orisha of Oyotunji Village.

15. Lionel F. Scott and Hermes Torres, *The Amber Talisman: Orisa in the New Millennium* (N.p.: Xlibris, 2003).

16. From Introduction to Yoruba Religion/Culture Saturday classes held at the home of a Yoruba priest of Oya in Brooklyn, New York, 2002.

17. See Elizabeth C. Fine and Jean Haskell Speer, eds., *Performance, Culture, and Identity* (Westport, Conn.: Praeger, 1992), 1–18.

18. Ibid., 9.

19. Epega and Neimark, *Sacred Ifa Oracle,* ix–x.

20. Ibid.

21. Stuart Hall's work on the theories of representation is helpful in understanding this concept. See "The Work of Representation," in *Representation: Cultural Representations and Signifying Practices,* ed. Stuart Hall (Thousand Oaks, Calif.: Sage, in association with the Open University, 1997), 24–26.

22. From 1999 to 2004, I observed and/or participated in several divination sessions with diviners in New York City and in South Carolina: initial consultation by phone, August 1999; subsequent consultations at Oyotunji Village, November 1999; roots reading, September 2001, in New York City; *Kofa ita* reading, March 2002, Oyotunji Village; consultation, June 2002, New York City; consultation, March 2004, Atlanta, Georgia. Between 2001 and 2004, I served as a recorder for a New York diviner on six different occasions. The names of the clients are confidential.

23. These classes were held in April and May 2002.

24. This approach is described at length by Robert S. Weiss, *Learning from Strangers: The Art and Method of Qualitative Interview Studies* (New York: Free Press, 1994), 45–51.

25. See D. Jean Clandinin and F. Michael Connelly, *Narrative Inquiry: Experience and Story in Qualitative Research* (San Francisco: Jossey-Bass, 2000).

26. Edward M. Bruner, ed., *Text, Play, and Story: The Construction and Reconstruction of Self and Society* (Prospect Heights, Ill.: Waveland Press, 1984).

27. Wande Abimbola, *Ifá: An Exposition of Ifá Literary Corpus* (New York: Athelia Henrietta Press, 1997), 115.

28. Ócha'ni Lele, *The Secrets of Afro-Cuban Divination: How to Cast the Diloggún, the Oracle of the Orishas* (Rochester, Vt.: Destiny Books, 2000).

29. Ibid., 12.

30. Ibid., 353–98.

31. Epega and Neimark, *Sacred Ifa Oracle,* ix–x, emphasis in original. Epega is a fifth-generation Nigerian babalawo, and Neimark is founder of the Ifa Foundation of North America.

32. Laura S. Grillo, "Divination in the Religious Systems of West Africa" (Ph.D. diss., University of Chicago, 1995).

33. Carl M. Hunt, *Oyotunji Village: The Yoruba Movement in America* (Washington, D.C.: University Press of America, 1979).

34. See Joseph M. Murphy, "Ritual Systems in Cuban Santería" (Ph.D. diss., Temple University, 1981). See also Murphy, *Santería: An African Religion in America* (Boston: Beacon Press, 1988), and George Edward Brandon, "The Dead Sell Memories: An Anthropological Study of Santeria in New York City" (Ph.D. diss., Rutgers University, 1983).

35. Mary Curry, *Making the Gods in New York: The Yoruba Religion in the African American Community* (New York: Garland, 1997).

36. Steven Gregory, *Santería in New York City: A Study in Cultural Resistance* (New York: Garland, 1999). Gregory's acknowledgment of the methodological challenges and ethical dilemmas posed by the secrecy that surrounds the religion and the obligations and responsibilities that come with access to ritual knowledge has been helpful in coping with issues of respect, reflexivity, sensitivity, and professionalism that are critical for ethnographers in this arena.

37. Maxine Kamari Clarke, *Mapping Yorùbá Networks: Power and Agency in the Making of Transnational Communities* (Durham: Duke University Press, 2004). Clark argues that the construction of "Yoruba traditions" at Oyotunji Village is a New World redemptive strategy engaged by a marginalized people in an effort to normalize history and identity.

38. Lionel F. Scott, *The Book of Ode: An Afrocentric View of Psychology and Religions* (N.p.: 1st Books Library, 2001). Scott, a licensed psychologist, writes about the orisha Ode, the Yoruba god of psychology, and argues for "Afrocentric therapeutic approaches and healing modalities."

39. See Awo Fá'lokun Fatunmbi, *Ìbà'ṣẹ Òrìṣà : Ifa Proverbs, Folktales, Sacred History, and Prayer* (Bronx, N.Y.: Original Publications, 1994).

40. Aina Olomo, *The Core of Fire: A Path to Yoruba Spiritual Activism* (Brooklyn, N.Y.: Athelia Henrietta Press, 2002), 156.

41. Ibid., 157.

42. Fine and Speer, *Performance, Culture, and Identity*, 16.

43. From my observations of an Ocha initiation ceremony and *ita* reading in Harlem, New York City, 2004. All interviewee responses to questions about the *ita* reading were consistent with this observation.

44. See Grillo, "Divination."

45. See W. B. Worthen, "Disciplines of the Text: Sites of Performance," in *The Performance Studies Reader*, ed. Henry Bial (New York: Routledge, 2004), 10–25.

Chapter 1

1. Sheree R. Thomas, *Dark Matter: Reading the Bones* (New York: Warner Books, 2004), ix.

2. Chief Adenibi S. Ajamu, minister of foreign affairs, Oyotunji Village, in discussion with the author, April 2004. Chief Ajamu is a babalawo.

3. Abimbola acknowledges E. R. Dennett, *Nigerian Studies; or, the Religious and Political System of the Yoruba* (London: Macmillan, 1910), as the source from which he gathered this material.

4. Abimbola acknowledges Samuel Johnson, *History of the Yoruba* (London: Routledge, 1921), as the source of this story.

5. Andrew Apter, *Black Critics and Kings: The Hermeneutics of Power in Yoruba Society* (Chicago: University of Chicago Press, 1992), 26.

6. Ibid.

7. See Fatunmbi, *Ìbà'ṣẹ Òrìṣà*, 44–45. Fatunmbi is active as a teacher/trainer in the United States. He established and maintains a website, http://www.awostudycenter.com, designed for the instruction of practitioners.

8. Ibid.

9. Consultations, interviews, and private conversations with a number of practitioners, along with my personal observations in New York City and Oyotunji Village, are the sources for this information.

10. Margaret Thompson Drewal, *Yoruba Ritual: Performers, Play, Agency* (Bloomington: Indiana University Press, 1992), 63–88.

11. From my observations of a birth reading conducted by Chief Ajamu in Atlanta, Georgia, March 2004.

12. From the author's observation of an Ocha (initiation ceremony in the Lucumi system) held in Harlem, May 2004.

13. Elizabeth M. Baeten, *The Magic Mirror: Myth's Abiding Power* (Albany: State University of New York Press, 1996).

14. Awo Fá'lokun Fatunmbi, *Awó: Ifá and the Theology of Orisha Divination* (Bronx, N.Y.: Original Publications, 1992), 19.

15. W. Abimbola, *Ifá*, 35–37.

16. J. Omosade Awolalu, *Yoruba Beliefs and Sacrificial Rites* (Brooklyn, N.Y.: Athelia Henrietta Press, 1996), 143.

17. Dr. Lionel F. Scott (Baba Odufora), in a private conversation with the author in April 2004, commented that he always performs the prescribed ebos before beginning the initiation ceremonies for a new initiate.

18. Oseijeman Adefunmi, *Olorisha: A Guidebook into Yoruba Religion*, Great Benin Books (Sheldon, S.C.: Orisha Academy, 1982), 7–9.

19. This chart is a compilation of information from the 2004 Yoruba Festival schedule published on the Oyotunji Village website (http://www.oyotunjivillage.net) and the founder's discussion of astrological energies and corresponding Orisha energies. See Adefunmi, *Olorisha*, 23.

20. While attending the Obatala Festival at Oyotunji Village in August 2003, I interviewed and/or met individuals from North Carolina, South Carolina, Georgia, Florida, Chicago, New York, Ohio, and Panama.

21. Ócha'ni Lele, *The Diloggún: The Orishas, Proverbs, Sacrifices, and Prohibitions of Cuban Santería* (Rochester, Vt.: Destiny Books, 2003), 9.

22. See also George Brandon, *Santeria from Africa to the New World: The Dead Sell Memories* (Bloomington: Indiana University Press, 1993), 71–77.

23. Several priests in New York recounted this story in interviews and private conversations in September 2003. See also Joseph M. Murphy, *Working the Spirit: Ceremonies of the African Diaspora* (Boston: Beacon Press, 1994), 81–82.

24. Brandon, *Santeria*, 104–20.

25. Hunt, *Oyotunji Village*; Clarke, *Mapping Yorùbá Networks*, 71–72; Curry, *Making the Gods*, 5–7.

26. Marta Moreno Vega, "The Candomblé and Eshu-Eleggua in Brazilian and Cuban Yoruba-Based Ritual," in *Black Theatre: Ritual Performance in the African Diaspora*, ed. Paul Carter Harrison, Victor Leo Walker II, and Gus Edwards (Philadelphia: Temple University Press, 2002), 153, 165.

27. W. E. B. Du Bois, *The Souls of Black Folk* (New York: Fawcett, 1961), 16–17.

28. Ọmọ́fọlábọ̀ S. Àjàyí, *Yoruba Dance: The Semiotics of Movement and Body Attitude in a Nigerian Culture* (Trenton, N.J.: Africa World Press, 1998), 43–57.

29. Ibid., 70.

30. Ibid., 92.

31. Anonymous orisha priest/drummer, conversation with the author, in Brooklyn, New York, summer 2003. See María Teresa Vélez, *Drumming for the Gods: The Life and Times of Felipe García Villamil, Santero, Palero, and Abakuá* (Philadelphia: Temple University Press, 2000), 39.

32. Georges Niangoran-Bouah, "The Talking Drum: A Traditional African Instrument of Liturgy and of Mediation of the Sacred," in *African Traditional Religions in Contemporary Society*, ed. Jacob K. Olupona (St. Paul, Minn.: Paragon House, 1991), 81.

33. Wande Abimbola, *Ifá Will Mend Our Broken World: Thoughts on Yoruba Religion and Culture in Africa and the Diaspora* (Roxbury, Mass.: Aim Books, 1997), 134.

34. Ibid., 134–38. See also Murphy, *Working the Spirit*, 104–9.

35. Vélez, *Drumming for the Gods*, 39.

36. W. Abimbola, *Ifá Will Mend Our Broken World*, 72.

37. Ibid., 75.

38. See Milton C. Sernett, *Afro-American Religious History: A Documentary Witness* (Durham: Duke University Press, 1985); Bruce Jackson, "The Other Kind of Doctor: Conjure and Magic in Black American Folk Medicine," in *African-American Religion: Interpretive Essays in History and Culture*, ed. Timothy E. Fulop and Albert J. Raboteau (New York: Routledge, 1997), 417–29; and Raboteau, *Slave Religion*.

39. "Henry Bibb: Conjuration and Witchcraft," in Sernett, *Afro-American Religious History*, 76.

40. Chief A. S. Ajamu, conversation with the author, Oyotunji Village, 2001.

41. Priestess of Oba, interview by author, tape recording, Abyssinian Baptist Church, following the Blue Nile rites of passage ceremony for young women, May 31, 2003.

42. From the "History" as published on the Abyssinian website (http://www.abyssinian.org), May 2003.

43. Rev. Violet L. Dease, private conversation with the author, Abyssinian Baptist Church, New York City, May 31, 2003.

44. I witnessed a procession of twelve to fifteen teenage participants in the rites of passage program organized by the Brooklyn Egbe Omo Yemonja (society). Participants dressed in white and wore multicolored stoles made of an African print. They carried a banner identifying the group as they processed along Far Rockaway Beach near Queens, New York, September 7, 2003.

Chapter 2

1. Paul Connerton, *How Societies Remember* (Cambridge: Cambridge University Press, 1989).

2. C. G. Jung, *The Archetypes and the Collective Unconscious*, 2nd ed., trans. R. F. C. Hull, vol. 9, pt. 1 of *The Collected Works* (Princeton: Princeton University Press, 1979–83), 90.

3. Arthur Flowers, *Mojo Rising: Confessions of a 21st Century Conjureman* (New York: Wanganegresse Press, 2001), 97.

4. Henry Louis Gates Jr. and Nellie Y. McKay, eds., *The Norton Anthology of African American Literature* (New York: Norton, 1996), 6. See also *Encyclopedia of African-American Culture and History*, ed. Jack Salzman, David L. Smith, and Cornel West (New York: Macmillan, 1996), s. v. "Music." Other sources include William Francis Allen, Charles P. Ware, and Lucy McKim Garrison, *Slave Songs of the United States* (New York: A. Simpson, 1867); Henry E. Krehbiel, *Afro-American Folksongs: A Study in Racial and National Music* (New York: G. Schirmer, 1915); John W. Work, *Folk Song of the American Negro* (Nashville: Fisk University Press, 1915); James Weldon Johnson and J. Rosamond Johnson, *The Books of American Negro Spirituals* (New York: Viking Press, 1925), and John Lovell, "The Social Implications of the Negro Spiritual," in *The Social Implications of Early Negro Music in the United States*, ed. Bernard Katz (New York: Arno Press, 1969).

5. Gates and McKay, *African American Literature*, 13.

6. Ibid.

7. Ibid., 11.

8. Jolande Jacobi, *Complex, Archetype, Symbol in the Psychology of C. G. Jung*, trans. Ralph Manheim (1959; Princeton: Princeton University Press, 1971), 103–10.

9. Lele, *Secrets*, 290–91, quoting Fatunmbi, *Awó*, 142.

10. James H. Cone, *The Spirituals and the Blues: An Interpretation* (Maryknoll, N.Y.: Orbis, 1972), 13.

11. Ibid., 26.

12. John Lovell Jr., *Black Song: The Forge and the Flame; The Story of How the Afro-American Spiritual Was Hammered Out* (New York: Macmillan, 1972), 126–33; see also Russell Ames, *The Story of American Folk Song* (New York: Grosset and Dunlap, 1960); B. A. Botkin, "The Folk-Say of Freedom Songs," *New Masses* 65 (October 21, 1947); and Oscar Brand, *The Ballad Mongers* (New York: Funk and Wagnalls, 1962).

13. Lovell underscores his point by referencing other analysts of folk songs, including Russell Ames. Ames described the spirituals as "sophisticated and ironic in meaning, classic and subtle in form," and he agreed with B. A. Botkin, who affirmed the irony of the spirituals and the blues, as well as Oscar Brand and Sidney Finkelstein, who wrote of the mask that disguised a yearning for freedom. See Lovell, *Black Song*, 191.

14. Ibid., 190.

15. Ibid., 138.

16. Samuel A. Floyd Jr., *The Power of Black Music: Interpreting Its History from Africa to the United States* (New York: Oxford University Press, 1995), 5–7.

17. Cone, *Spirituals*, 105.

18. Homi K. Bhabha, *The Location of Culture* (New York: Routledge, 1994), 18.

19. Cone, *Spirituals*, 124.

20. Robert Farris Thompson, *Flash of the Spirit: African and Afro-American Art and Philosophy* (New York: Vintage Books, 1983), 53.

21. I personally received an Ogun "pot" containing such objects in a ceremony performed by a babalawo from Oyotunji Village in March 2003.

22. Gary Edwards and John Mason, *Black Gods: Òrìṣà Studies in the New World* (Brooklyn, N.Y.: Yoruba Theological Archministry), 23.

23. Sandra T. Barnes, "The Many Faces of *Ogun:* Introduction to the First Edition," in *Africa's Ogun: Old World and New*, ed. Sandra T. Barnes (Bloomington: Indiana University Press, 1997), 16–20.

24. Cone, *Spirituals*, 121.

25. Lele, *Secrets*, 91–92.

26. Floyd, *Power*, 76.

27. Ibid., 91.

28. Ibid., 74.

29. Gates and McKay, *African American Literature*, 24.

30. Ademola, interview by author, tape recording, Brooklyn, New York, September 7, 2003.

31. Ibid. These ideas were also expressed by an Oshun priestess, interview by author, tape recording, Oyotunji Village, May 23, 2003, as well as in *The Orisha Tradition: An African Worldview* (New York: Caribbean Cultural Center, 1991), videocassette.

32. Gates and McKay, *African American Literature*, 29.

33. Joseph M. Murphy and Mei-Mei Sanford, eds., *Ọṣun Across the Waters: A Yoruba Goddess in Africa and the Americas* (Bloomington: Indiana University Press, 2001), 8.

34. George Brandon, "Ochun in the Bronx," in Murphy and Sanford, *Ọṣun Across the Waters*, 163.

35. Rachel Elizabeth Harding, "'What Part of the River You're In': African American Women in Devotion to Òsun," in Murphy and Sanford, *Ọṣun Across the Waters*, 166.

36. Lele, *Secrets*, 138.

37. Angela Y. Davis, *Blues Legacies and Black Feminism: Gertrude "Ma" Rainey, Bessie Smith, and Billie Holiday* (New York: Pantheon Books, 1998), 74.

38. Edwards and Mason, *Black Gods,* 92.

39. *Africana: The Encyclopedia of the African and African American Experience,* ed. Kwame Anthony Appiah and Henry Louis Gates Jr. (New York: Basic Civitas Books, 1999), s.v. "Black Consciousness in the United States," "Black Arts Movement," "Black Power," and "Black Panther Party."

40. Dr. Lionel F. Scott (Baba Odufora), a priest of Obatala, conversation with the author, New York City, September 6, 2003.

41. Chief Adeyemi, conversation with the author, Oyotunji Village, August 2003.

42. George Breitma, ed., *Malcolm X Speaks: Selected Speeches and Statements* (New York: Pathfinder, 1989), 38–40.

43. Ibid., 23–44. See also Malcolm X, "The Ballot or the Bullet," Online Speech Bank (http://www.americanrhetoric.com).

44. From a videotaped discussion held in 1995 at the Caribbean Cultural Center, New York City.

45. Adefunmi, *Olorisa,* III.

46. Lele, *Secrets,* 206.

Chapter 3

1. Vincent L. Wimbush, ed., *African Americans and the Bible: Sacred Texts and Social Textures* (New York: Continuum, 2000), 29.

2. From an interview with a young priest of Obatala currently residing in Chicago. The interview was conducted at Oyotunji Village, August 2003.

3. HRG Iyashanla, conversation with the author, Oyotunji Village, August 27, 2000.

4. Fatunmbi, *Ìbà'ṣẹ Òrìṣà,* 40.

5. Fatunmbi's work appears to be widely read among practitioners. It is also controversial.

6. This paradigm is discussed at length in Wimbush's introductory essay cited above. He draws from Ishmael Reed's "Neo-HooDoo Manifesto" (1972) for the terms "mumbo jumbo" and "neo-hoodoo."

7. Clyde W. Ford, *The Hero with an African Face: Mythic Wisdom of Traditional Africa* (New York: Bantam Books, 1999), viii–ix.

8. Ibid.

9. Ibid.

10. Scott and Torres, *Amber Talisman,* 53.

11. Anonymous graduate student, conversation with the author, New York City, June 2002.

12. John Mbiti, *African Religions and Philosophy* (Garden City, N.Y.: Anchor Books, 1970), 233, cited by Philip M. Peek in *African Divination Systems: Ways of Knowing* (Bloomington: Indiana University Press, 1991), 193.

13. Private conversation with New York priest, 2002.

14. Scott and Torres, *Amber Talisman,* 14.

15. Frederick J. Ruf, *Entangled Voices: Genre and the Religious Construction of the Self* (New York: Oxford University Press, 1997).

16. John Mason, *Orin Òrìṣà: Songs for Selected Heads* (Brooklyn, N.Y.: Yoruba Theological Archministry, 1992), 7.

17. Yemonja priestess, Brooklyn, New York, August 2003.

18. See Ruf's discussion of the lyric voice in *Entangled Voices.*

19. The ethnographer's description becomes a kind of interpretive "reading" of a cultural text, a signifying practice in itself; see Clifford Geertz, *The Interpretation of Cultures* (New York: Basic Books, 1973), 3–30.

20. Ruf, drawing on Don Ihde's concept of the "phenomenology of voice," discusses contextuality, sociality, and embodiment as aspects of the presence created by voice. See Ruf, *Entangled Voices.*

21. Scott and Torres, *Amber Talisman,* 57.

22. Michael Atwood Mason discusses this concept and cites Edward L. Schieffelin's "Performance and the Cultural Construction of Reality," *American Ethnologist* 12, no. 4 (1985): 707–24.

23. Scott and Torres, *Amber Talisman,* 39.

Chapter 4

1. Schieffelin, "Performance," 707–24.

2. Preucel, *Archaeological Semiotics,* 45.

3. Notes from Yoruba Religion/Culture Study Group Ile (house) of Shango of the Nine Winds, Brooklyn, New York, 2002. I attended this group as a participant observer.

4. Ford, *Hero,* 145.

5. Wole Soyinka, *Myth, Literature, and the African World* (London: Cambridge University Press, 1976), 1.

6. Ibid., 29–30.

7. Drewal, *Yoruba Ritual,* 63–87.

8. In this discussion, Drewal cites Victor Turner's explanation of the tripartite movement found in ritual process as a heuristic tool for understanding the rite of passage ritual as a journey that evokes personal transformation. See Victor Turner, *The Ritual Process: Structure and Anti-Structure* (Ithaca: Cornell University Press, 1977), 94.

9. Drewal, *Yoruba Ritual,* 52–62.

10. Ford, *Hero,* 4.

11. Ibid., 6.

12. This adaptation of Scott and Torres's narration of "The Magic Amber" is cited at length here in order to provide the fullest sense of the role of mythic oral text in the Orisha tradition.

13. See William G. Doty, "Questions to Address to Mythic Texts," in *Mythography: The Study of Myths and Rituals* (Tuscaloosa: University of Alabama Press, 2000), 466–67. Doty also asks questions about the psychological aspects of the mythic text (both individual and communal) as well as its literary, symbolic, and iconographic features, which I will address below.

14. Lele, *Secrets,* 205–20, 378.

15. New York priest of Obatala, phone conversation with the author, 2003.

16. These sentiments were expressed by Yoruba priests, both in New York City and in Oyotunji Village, in private conversations during participant observation research in 2002.

17. Scott and Torres, *Amber Talisman,* 29–30.

18. Hunt, *Oyotunji Village,* v–viii.

19. Ibid., 36.

20. Ibid.

21. Ibid., 41.

22. Chief A. S. Ajamu, conversation with the author, Oyotunji Village, October 13, 2000.

23. Connerton, *How Societies Remember,* 1–5.

24. Hunt, *Oyotunji Village,* 40.

25. Ibid.

26. Ibid.

27. Ibid.

28. Mechal Sobel, *Trabelin' On: The Slave Journey to an Afro-Baptist Faith* (Princeton: Princeton University Press, 1979).

29. Raboteau, *Slave Religion.*

30. Vincent L. Wimbush, *The Bible and African Americans: A Brief History* (Minneapolis: Fortress Press, 2003).

31. See Fine and Speer, *Performance, Culture, and Identity,* 1–23.

32. Ibid., 16.

33. Yemonja priestess, conversation with the author, Brooklyn, New York, June 10, 2003.

34. Obatala priestess, interview with the author, May 23, 2003, New York City. This priestess of Obatala was born into the religion and was initiated at age four because of health issues.

35. Adefunmi, *Olorisha,* v.

36. Sernett, *Afro-American Religious History.*

37. Timothy E. Fulop and Albert J. Raboteau, eds., *African American Religion: Interpretive Essays in History and Culture* (New York: Routledge, 1997).

38. Anthony B. Pinn, *Varieties of African American Religious Experience* (Minneapolis: Fortress Press, 1998), 1. Here Pinn quotes from his previous work, *Why, Lord?: Suffering and Evil in Black Theology* (New York: Continuum, 1995), 20.

39. Pinn is right in his critique of the focus and scope of black theology. James H. Cone and Gayraud S. Wilmore's two-volume collection *Black Theology: A Documentary History* (Maryknoll, N.Y.: Orbis Books, 1993), is one example of a work focusing solely on Christianity. Pinn makes an important contribution to expanding the conversation through *Varieties of African American Religious Experience.*

40. Fine and Speer, *Performance, Culture, and Identity,* 10.

41. Wimbush, *Bible and African Americans,* 29.

Chapter 5

1. Field notes from a participant observation scene at Oyotunji Village, March 3, 2002. Here, I was the client receiving the *ita* reading, a reading done as part of one's formal entrance into the religion.

2. Teresa N. Washington, *Our Mothers, Our Powers, Our Texts: Manifestations of Àjẹ́ in Africana Literature* (Bloomington: Indiana University Press, 2005), 90.

3. Ibid., 38, 90, 108–109.

4. Priest of Obatala, conversation with the author, New York City, May 2003.

5. Anonymous African American woman, an *aleyo* (uninitiated person) who lives in Atlanta, Georgia, in a conversation with the author following a reading from a diviner at Oyotunji Village, December 26, 2000.

6. Wande Abimbola, "Images of Women in the Ifa Literary Corpus," in *Queens, Queen Mothers, Priestesses, and Power: Case Studies in African Gender,* ed. Flora Edouwaye S. Kaplan (New York: New York Academy of Sciences, 1997), 402–3.

7. Ibid., 403.

8. Ibid.

9. Olomo, *Core of Fire,* 124.

10. Washington, *Our Mothers, Our Powers,* 6–7. It is important to note that expressions of aje are not limited to persons of Yoruba ancestry. The African American descendants of the enslaved Africans in Mississippi and Louisiana, as noted earlier, came from a diversity of ethnic groups.

11. Luisah Teish, *Jambalaya: The Natural Woman's Book of Personal Charms and Practical Rituals* (San Francisco: Harper and Row, 1985). One chapter is devoted to each of the nine activities.

12. Ibid., 46–48.

13. Patricia Hill Collins, *Black Feminist Thought: Knowledge, Consciousness, and the Politics of Empowerment* (New York: Routledge, 1990).

14. Ibid., 32.

15. Teish, *Jambalaya*, 47–48.

16. Collins, *Black Feminist Thought*, 224. Collins also acknowledges the presence of these concepts in the scholarly work of other black feminists, including Audre Lorde, *Sister Outsider: Essays and Speeches* (Trumansburg, N.Y.: Crossing Press, 1984); Filomina Chioma Steady, "The Black Woman Cross-Culturally: An Overview," in *The Black Woman Cross-Culturally*, edited by Filomina Chioma Steady (Cambridge, Mass.: Schenkman, 1987); Angela Y. Davis, *Women, Culture, and Politics* (New York: Random House, 1989); and bell hooks, *Talking Back: Thinking Feminist, Thinking Black* (Boston: South End Press, 1989).

17. Collins, *Black Feminist Thought*, 222.

18. Teish, *Jambalaya*, 251.

19. Ibid., 63. Teish uses an alternative spelling for *ashe*.

20. Ibid., 62.

21. Olomo, *Core of Fire*, 161.

22. Ibid..

23. See bell hooks, *Sisters of the Yam: Black Women and Self-Recovery* (Boston: South End Press, 1993), 8.

24. Cited in ibid., 9.

25. Her vivid description is worth quoting here: "black female students would . . . confess the truth of their lives—that they were terrorized psychologically by low self-esteem; that they were the victims of rape, incest, and domestic violence; that they lived in fear of being unmasked as the inferiors of their white peers; that stress was making their hair fall out; that every other month one of them was attempting suicide; that they were anorexic, bulimic, or drug addicted."

26. The yam is a staple of the traditional Yoruba diet. It is also a ritual food often prepared for offerings to Yemonja as well as other orisha. See John Mason, *Ìdáná Fún Òrìṣà: Cooking for Selected Heads* (Brooklyn, N.Y.: Yoruba Theological Archministry, 1999), 126, 142.

27. Ibid., 8.

28. See, for example, the works of Olomo and Teish, along with the remarks of participants in this study.

29. Washington, *Our Mothers, Our Powers*.

Chapter 6

1. Murphy and Sanford, *Ọ̀ṣun Across the Waters*, 2.

2. Edwards and Mason, *Black Gods*, 98–101.

3. Awo Fá'lokun Fatunmbi, *Oshun: Ifá and the Spirit of the River* (Bronx, N.Y.: Original Publications, 1993), 5–7. Other versions of this same story appear in much of the literature on Oshun. For example, see "The Bag of Wisdom: *Oshun* and the Origins of the Ifa Divination," by Wande Abimbola, in Murphy and Sanford, *Ọ̀ṣun Across the Waters*, 141–54.

4. Fatunmbi, *Oshun*, 7.

5. Rowland Abiodun, "Hidden Power: Ọ̀ṣun, the Seventeenth Odù," in Murphy and Sanford, *Ọ̀ṣun Across the Waters,* 16–18.

6. Ibid.

7. Rowland Abiodun, "Who Was the First to Speak? Insights from Ifá Orature and Sculptural Repertoire," in *Òrìṣà Devotion as World Religion: The Globalization of Yorùbá Religious Culture,* ed. Jacob K. Olupona and Terry Rey (Madison: University of Wisconsin Press, 2008), 16–18.

8. Doty, *Mythography,* 467.

9. Abiodun, "Hidden Power," 29.

10. Catherine Bell, *Ritual Perspectives and Dimensions* (New York: Oxford University Press, 1997), 81.

11. Example provided by a New York priest of Obatala who has initiated more than sixty individuals. This part of the initiation ceremony is conducted privately. Information provided in a telephone conversation, January 2005.

12. From a private conversation with a New York priest of Oshun, January 2005.

13. Oyeronke Oyewumi, "The Translations of Cultures: Engendering Yoruba Language, Orature, and World-Sense," in *Women, Gender, Religion: A Reader,* ed. Elizabeth A. Castelli (New York: Palgrave, 2001), 76.

14. Ibid., 77.

15. There is, however, a Women's Society responsible for training young women at Oyotunji Village. The details regarding the scope and content of such training are available only to fully initiated practitioners. I was, therefore, unable to ascertain the extent to which gender-specific roles are a part of the training.

16. Oyeronke Olajubu, *Women in the Yoruba Religious Sphere* (Albany: State University of New York Press, 2003), 21.

17. Ibid., 22.

18. Ibid.; Olajubu is quoting Apter, *Black Critics and Kings.*

19. Dr. Lionel F. Scott, psychologist and priest of Obatala, private conversation with the author, New York City, 2001.

20. Priest of Oshun, conversation with the author, Brooklyn, New York, September 2003. He grew up in the religion and was formally initiated as a priest of Oshun in 1997.

21. Priest of Oshun, conversation with the author, Oyotunji Village, August 2003. He was initiated in 1986.

22. John Mason, private conversation with the author, New York, September 2003. I spoke with him during the Yemonja Festival.

23. Priest of Obatala, interview by the author, Oyotunji Village, August 23, 2003.

24. Dr. Lionel F. Scott (Baba Odufora) in a talk given during an informal short course, Introduction to Yoruba Religion/Culture, Brooklyn, New York, April 6, 2002. Also see Edwards and Mason, *Black Gods,* 85–89.

25. Scott, talk during Introduction to Yoruba Religion/Culture.

26. Lloyd Weaver and Olurunmi Egbelade, "Ese Five," in *Maternal Divinity, Yemonja: Tranquil Sea, Turbulent Tides; Eleven Yoruba Tales,* ed. Weaver and Egbelade (Brooklyn, N.Y.: Athelia Henrietta Press, 1999), 99–115. This *apataki* is an abbreviated version of *ese* five.

27. Priestess of Yemonja, conversation with the author during an Oche ceremony in New York City, May 2003.

28. New York priestess of Yemonja, conversation with the author while attending the Obatala festival at Oyotunji Village, August 2002.

29. Priest of Yemonja, conversation with the author, New York City, 2002.

30. Priestess of Yemonja from Brooklyn, New York, in an interview with the author while attending the Obatala Festival, Oyotunji Village, August 2002.

31. Priestess of Yemonja, conversation with the author, Brooklyn, New York, June 2003.

32. Luisah Teish told this story during her presentation on embedded knowledge at the Pagan Studies Conference, Claremont Graduate University, Claremont, California, January 23, 2005.

33. Ibid.

34. Sheila S. Walker, *Ceremonial Spirit Possession in America and Afro-America: Forms, Meanings, and Functional Significance for Individuals and Social Groups* (Leiden: E. J. Brill, 1972), 149–50.

35. Teish, *Jambalaya,* 111.

36. Ibid., 119.

37. Ibid.

38. Unpublished notes from a class taught in Brooklyn, New York, in March 2002 by orisha priest Lionel Scott.

39. Priest of Obatala, interview with the author, Oyotunji Village, August 23, 2003.

40. Lele, *Secrets,* 395.

41. Ibid.

42. Teish, *Jambalaya,* 120–21.

43. Ibid., 47. Teish defines "Woman Spirit Movement" as women who seek to create a tradition other than the patriarchal religions.

44. Marcus Garvey, writing from Atlanta Prison, February 10, 1925, as quoted in Kuwasi Balagoon et al., *Look for Me in the Whirlwind: The Collective Autobiography of the New York 21* (New York: Random House, 1971).

45. *Webster's New World Dictionary, Second College Edition* (Cleveland: William Collins and World Publishing, 1976), 1620.

46. Judith Gleason, *Oya: In Praise of the Goddess* (Boston: Shambhala, 1987), 11.

47. Luisah Teish, "Carnival of the Spirit—Oya," *Oya N'Soro: Oya Speaks! An Explorative E-Zine of Orisha/Ifa Understanding* 2, no. 2 (2004). Retrieved from http://oyansoro.com/archives/ArchivesOyansoro/11_04/articles/oya.htm.

Conclusion

1. See Vincent L. Wimbush, ed., *Theorizing Scriptures: New Critical Orientations to a Cultural Phenomenon* (New Brunswick: Rutgers University Press, 2008), 14–15.

2. Herbert J. Rubin and Irene S. Rubin, *Qualitative Interviewing: The Art of Hearing Data,* 2nd ed. (Thousand Oaks, Calif.: Sage, 2005), vii.

3. Robert Atkinson, *The Gift of Stories: Practical and Spiritual Applications of Autobiography, Life Stories, and Personal Mythmaking* (Westport, Conn.: Bergin and Garvey, 1995), 107.

4. Ibid., 3.

5. Joan Wink, *Critical Pedagogy: Notes from the Real World* (New York: Longman, 2000), 56–57.

6. Norman K. Denzin, *Performance Ethnography: Critical Pedagogy and the Politics of Culture* (Thousand Oaks, Calif.: Sage, 2003), 12.

7. Ibid., 13.

8. My own poetic description based on Gates's discussion of Esu. See Gates, *Signifying Monkey.*

9. Denzin, *Performance Ethnography,* 13.

10. Ibid., 13–14.

11. Randall T. G. Hill, "Performance Pedagogy Across the Curriculum," in Dailey, *Future of Performance Studies,* 143. In a similar manner, Elizabeth Bell suggests that the performance model "shifts the burden of locating 'meaning' from the postmodern text to the performer and teaches that performance is always a pleasurable and dangerous accountability—not to 'certainties' in the text, or to authorial intention, or to canonical tradition, but—to the 'spin' put on it." See Bell, "Accessing the Power to Signify: Learning to Read in Performance Studies," in Dailey, *Future of Performance Studies,* 59.

12. Carol L. Benton, "Performance Studies Across the Curriculum: Using Performance in Introduction to Women's Studies; A Case Study," in Dailey, *Future of Performance Studies,* 145–149.

13. See Paulo Freire, *Pedagogy of Hope: Reliving "Pedagogy of the Oppressed"* (New York: Continuum, 1998).

14. Musa Dube presenting at Scripps College, Claremont, California, for AIDS Awareness Week, March 2005. See also Musa W. Dube, ed., *Other Ways of Reading: African Women and the Bible* (Atlanta: Society of Biblical Literature, 2001).

15. Katie G. Cannon, "Structured Academic Amnesia: As If This True Womanist Story Never Happened," in *Deeper Shades of Purple: Womanism in Religion and Society,* ed. Stacey M. Floyd Thomas (New York: New York University Press, 2006), 2526.

SELECTED BIBLIOGRAPHY

Abimbola, Wande. *Ifá: An Exposition of Ifá Literary Corpus*. New York: Athelia Henrietta Press, 1997.

Abiodun, Rowland. "Who Was the First to Speak? Insights from Ifa Orature and Sculptural Repertoire." In *Òrìṣà Devotion as World Religion: The Globalization of Yorùbá Religious Culture,* edited by Jacob K. Olupona and Terry Rey. Madison: University of Wisconsin Press, 2008.

Apter, Andrew. *Black Critics and Kings: The Hermeneutics of Power in Yoruba Society*. Chicago: University of Chicago Press, 1992.

Azibo, Daudi Ajani ya. *African Psychology in Historical Perspective*. Trenton, N.J.: Africa World Press, 1996.

Baer, Hans A., and Merrill Singer. *African American Religion in the Twentieth Century*. Knoxville: University of Tennessee Press, 1992.

Bal, Mieke, Jonathan Crewe, and Leo Spitzer, eds. *Acts of Memory: Cultural Recall in the Present*. Hanover: University Press of New England, 1999.

Barber, Karen, and P. F. de Mores Farias. *Discourse and Disguises: The Interpretation of African Oral Texts*. Birmingham, U.K.: University of Birmingham, Centre of West African Studies, 1989.

Bascom, William. *Ifa Divination: Communication Between Gods and Men in West Africa*. Bloomington: Indiana University Press, 1969.

———. *Sixteen Cowries: Yoruba Divination from Africa to the New World*. Bloomington: Indiana University Press, 1980.

Bauman, Richard. *Verbal Art as Performance*. Prospect Heights, Ill.: Waveland Press, 1977.

Bell, Catherine. *Ritual Theory, Ritual Practice*. New York: Oxford University Press, 1992.

Ben-Amos, Dan, and Liliane Weissberg, eds. *Cultural Memory and the Construction of Identity*. Detroit, Mich.: Wayne State University Press, 1999.

Brandon, George. *Santeria from Africa to the New World: The Dead Sell Memories*. Bloomington: Indiana University Press, 1993.

Brown, Karen McCarthy. *Mama Lola: A Vodou Priestess in Brooklyn*. Berkeley: University of California Press, 1991.

Bruner, Edward M., ed. *Text, Play, and Story: The Construction and Reconstruction of Self and Society*. Prospect Heights, Ill.: Waveland Press, 1984.

Bruner, Edward M., and Victor Turner, eds. *The Anthropology of Experience*. Chicago: University of Illinois Press, 1986.

Clandinin, D. Jean, and F. Michael Connelly. *Narrative Inquiry: Experience and Story in Qualitative Research*. San Francisco: Jossey-Bass, 2000.

Connerton, Paul. *How Societies Remember*. Cambridge: Cambridge University Press, 1989.

Conniff, Michael L., and Thomas J. Davis. *Africans in the Americas: A History of the Black Diaspora*. New York: St. Martin's Press, 1994.

Conquergood, Dwight. "Beyond the Texts: Toward a Performative Cultural Politics." In The *Future of Performance Studies: Visions and Revisions,* edited by Sheron J. Dailey. Annandale, Va.: National Communication Association, 1998.

———. "Rethinking Ethnography: Towards A Critical Cultural Politics." *Communication Monographs* 58 (June 1991).

Crocker, J. Christopher, and David J. Sapir. *The Social Use of Metaphor: Essays on the Anthropology of Rhetoric.* Philadelphia: University of Pennsylvania Press, 1977.

Curry, Mary. *Making the Gods in New York: The Yoruba Religion in the African American Community.* New York: Garland, 1997.

Curtin, Philip D. *Africa Remembered: Narratives by West Africans from the Era of the Slave Trade.* Madison: University of Wisconsin Press, 1967.

Denzin, Norman K. *Performance Ethnography: Critical Pedagogy and the Politics of Culture.* Thousand Oaks, Calif.: Sage, 2003.

Dey, Ian. *Grounding Grounded Theory: Guidelines for Qualitative Inquiry.* San Diego: Academic Press, 1999.

Doty, William. *Mythography: The Study of Myths and Rituals.* Tuscaloosa: University of Alabama Press, 2000.

Drake, St. Clair. *The Redemption of Africa and Black Religion.* Chicago: Third World Press, 1970.

Drewal, Margaret Thompson. *Yoruba Ritual: Performers, Play, Agency.* Bloomington: Indiana University Press, 1992.

Durkheim, Emile. *The Elementary Forms of Religious Life.* 1915. New York: Free Press, 1965.

Edwards, Gary, and John Mason. *Black Gods: Òrìṣà Studies in the New World.* Brooklyn, N.Y.: Yoruba Theological Archministry, 1998.

Epega, Afolabi A., and Philip John Neimark. *The Sacred Ifa Oracle.* Brooklyn, N.Y.: Athelia Henrietta Press, 1995.

Fine, Elizabeth C., and Jean Haskell Speer, eds. *Performance, Culture, and Identity.* Westport, Conn.: Praeger, 1992.

Ford, Clyde W. *The Hero with an African Face: Mythic Wisdom of Traditional Africa.* New York: Bantam Books, 1999.

Freire, Paulo, and Donaldo P. Macedo. *Literacy: Reading the Word and the World.* London: Routledge, 1987.

Fulop, Timothy E., and Albert J. Raboteau, eds. *African-American Religion: Interpretive Essays in History and Culture.* New York: Routledge, 1997.

Geertz, Clifford. *The Interpretation of Cultures.* New York: Basic Books, 1973.

Graham, William A. *Beyond the Written Word: Oral Aspects of Scripture in the History of Religion.* Cambridge: Cambridge University Press, 1987.

Gregory, Steven. *Santería in New York City: A Study in Cultural Resistance.* New York: Garland, 1999.

Grillo, Laura S. "Divination in the Religious Systems of West Africa." Ph.D. diss., University of Chicago, 1995.

Halbwachs, Maurice. *On Collective Memory.* Edited and translated by Lewis A. Coser. Chicago: University of Chicago Press, 1992.

Hall, Stuart, ed. *Representation: Cultural Representations and Signifying Practices.* Thousand Oaks, Calif.: Sage, in association with the Open University, 1997.

Hervieu-Léger, Danièle. *Religion as a Chain of Memory.* New Brunswick: Rutgers University Press, 2000.

Huberman, Michael, and Matthew B. Miles. "Data Management and Analysis Methods." In *Collecting and Interpreting Qualitative Materials,* edited by Norman K. Denzin and Yvonna S. Lincoln. Thousand Oaks, Calif.: Sage, 1988.

Hunt, Carl M. *Oyotunji Village: The Yoruba Movement in America.* Washington, D.C.: University Press of America, 1979.

Lele, Ócha'ni. *Obí: Oracle of Cuban Santería.* Rochester, Vt.: Destiny Books, 2001.

———. *The Secrets of Afro-Cuban Divination: How to Cast the Diloggún, the Oracle of the Orishas.* Rochester, Vt.: Destiny Books, 2000.

Levering, Miriam, ed. *Rethinking Scripture: Essays from a Comparative Perspective.* Albany: State University of New York Press, 1989.

Long, Charles H. *Significations: Signs, Symbols, and Images in the Interpretation of Religion.* Philadelphia: Fortress Press, 1986.

Mason, Michael Atwood. *Living Santería: Rituals and Experiences in an Afro-Cuban Religion.* Washington, D.C.: Smithsonian Institute Press, 2002.

Mbiti, John. *African Religions and Philosophy.* Garden City, N.Y.: Anchor Books, 1970.

McCartney, John. *Black Power Ideologies: An Essay in African-American Political Thought.* Philadelphia: Temple University Press, 1992.

Murphy, Joseph M. *Working the Spirit: Ceremonies of the African Diaspora.* Boston: Beacon Press, 1994.

Ngũgĩ wa Thion'go. *Decolonizing the Mind: The Politics of Language in African Literature.* Oxford: James Currey, 2003.

Olupona, Jacob K., ed. *African Traditional Religions in Contemporary Society.* St. Paul, Minn.: Paragon House, 1991.

Olupona, Jacob K., and Terry Rey, eds. *Òrìṣà Devotion as World Religion: The Globalization of Yorùbá Religious Culture.* Madison: University of Wisconsin Press, 2008.

Peek, Philip M. *African Divination Systems: Ways of Knowing.* Bloomington: Indiana University Press, 1991.

Peel, J. D. Y. *Religious Encounter and the Making of the Yoruba.* Bloomington: Indiana University Press, 2000.

Preucel, Robert W. *Archaeological Semiotics.* Malden, Mass.: Wiley-Blackwell, 2010.

Price, Sally. *Co-Wives and Calabashes.* Ann Arbor: University of Michigan Press, 1984.

Proust, Marcel. *Remembrance of Things Past.* New York: Random House, 1981.

Raboteau, Albert J. *Slave Religion: The "Invisible Institution" in the Antebellum South.* Updated ed. New York: Oxford University Press, 2004.

Ruf, Frederick J. *Entangled Voices: Genre and the Religious Construction of the Self.* New York: Oxford University Press, 1997.

Said, Edward W. *Culture and Imperialism.* New York: Vintage Books, 1994.

Schechner, Richard. *Performance Studies: An Introduction.* London: Routledge, 2002.

Scott, James C. *Domination and the Acts of Resistance: Hidden Transcripts.* New Haven: Yale University Press, 1990.

Scott, Lionel F., and Hermes Torres-Ifaraba. *The Amber Talisman: Orisa in the New Millennium.* N.p.: Xlibris, 2003.

Sernett, Milton C. *Afro-American Religious History: A Documentary Witness.* Durham: Duke University Press, 1985.

Shaughnessy, James D. *The Roots of Ritual.* Grand Rapids, Mich.: Eerdmans, 1973.

Smith, Linda T. *Decolonizing Methodologies: Research and Indigenous Peoples.* London: Zed Books, 2005.

Smith, William Cantwell. *What Is Scripture? A Comparative Perspective.* Minneapolis: Fortress Press, 1993.

Soyinka, Wole. *Myth, Literature, and the African World.* London: Cambridge University Press, 1976.

Thandeka. *Learning to Be White: Money, Race, and God in America.* New York: Continuum, 2000.

Vega, Marta Moreno. *The Altar of My Soul: The Living Traditions of Santería.* New York: One World, 2000.

Wagner, Roy. *The Invention of Culture.* Chicago: University of Chicago Press, 1975.

Washington, Teresa N. *Our Mothers, Our Powers, Our Texts: Manifestations of Àjẹ́ in Africana Literature.* Bloomington: Indiana University Press, 2005.

Weiss, Robert S. *Learning from Strangers: The Art and Method of Qualitative Interview Studies*. New York: Free Press, 1994.

Wilmore, Gayraud S. *Black Religion and Black Radicalism: An Interpretation of the Religious History of Afro-American People*. New York: Orbis Books, 1983.

Wimbush, Vincent L., ed. *African Americans and the Bible: Sacred Texts and Social Textures*. New York: Continuum, 2000.

———. *The Bible and African Americans: A Brief History*. Minneapolis: Fortress Press, 2003.

———. *Theorizing Scriptures: New Critical Orientations to a Cultural Phenomenon*. New Brunswick: Rutgers University Press, 2008.

Zuesse, Evan M. *Ritual Cosmos: The Sanctification of Life in African Religions*. Athens: Ohio University Press, 1979.

INDEX

www.ingramcontent.com/pod-product-compliance
Ingram Content Group UK Ltd.
Pitfield, Milton Keynes, MK11 3LW, UK
UKHW040050250726
473705UK00001B/25

9 780271 054063